THE WRITER IN THE WRITING

Author as Hero in Postwar American Fiction

Krzysztof Andrzejczak

International Scholars Publications
San Francisco - London - Bethesda
1999

Library of Congress Cataloging-in-Publication Data

Andrzejczak, Krzysztof, 1942-
    The writer in the writing : author as hero in postwar American
    fiction / Krzysztof Andrzejczak.
      p. cm.
    Originally published: Lódz : Wydawnictwo Uniwersytetu Lódzkiego,
    1996
    Based on the author's thesis.
    Includes bibliographical references and index.
    ISBN 1-57309- 282-7 (alk. paper)
    1. American fiction--20th century--History and criticism.
    2. Autobiographical fiction, American--History and criticism.
    3. Authorship in literature. 4. Authors in literature. 5. Heroes
    in literature. 6. Self in literature. I. Title.
    PS374.A88A86   1998
    813' .54093528--dc21   98-15063

Editorial Inquiries:
International Scholars Publications
7831 Woodmont Avenue, #345
Bethesda, MD 20814

To order: (800) 55-PUBLISH

For my mother
Irena Andrzejczak
1914-1990

CONTENTS

PREFACE

The impulse of "turning writers into heroes...has become more pronounced than ever," Michiko Kakutani observes in the early 1980s.[1] Indeed, recent decades bring so many prominent novels in which protagonists are writers that we can not only speak of the re-emergence of the writer as hero in American fiction, but of a new fascination with the *Künstlerroman*, a massive vogue, a modern allegory. The writer figure in contemporary fiction appears as a paragon of verbal dexterity, intellectual exuberance and financial success. He recognizes, with a new sense of excitement and imagination, that he can use his craft to re-shape experience, to fill fictional situations with multifarious authorial selves, or to reveal new uses of language.

The American need for self-study and self-expression is, no doubt, reflected in this phenomenon. Publishing a book has become a foremost social distinction and an inalienable right in "the culture of narcissism." To express oneself in print is a license to announce options, to have an audience, to present one's own version of the American experience, or history - as well as to gain publicity, glamor and money. Millions of Americans aspire to write about themselves, to become authors, to be published. "I wanted to be a writer. Didn't everybody?," mused Patricia Hampl, in *A Romantic Education*, even before she went to college. "Because writing, I sensed, *let you in*; it subsumed these other things, oceans and microscopes, teachers, dining room tables."[2]

Most of those who publish bestsellers are soon eclipsed or forgotten because thousands of similarly experienced, bold or inspired authors are eager for their "fifteen minutes of fame." Yet a celebrated group of authors occupies a special niche in American awareness. They are lavishly rewarded, glamorized by the media and indulged by academic institutions and the centers of power. They are seen as mythic figures, unusually talented formulators of vital visions and insights. "If I marry *anybody*, I'll marry a writer," says a young woman to Garp, in John Irving's *The World According to Garp*. Then she adds: "a real writer." Consequently, Garp decides "he was going to be a writer. A *real* writer...."[3]

Literary fame is seductive and addictive, and writer heroes gladly speak of their lust for success. Upon achieving it, they highlight and amplify their celebrity. Much of Saul Bellow's massive *Humboldt's Gift* deals with the elation and confusion of becoming a literary luminary in America. To Charlie Citrine, the new status as a major writer is like "picking up a dangerous wire fatal to ordinary folk," like "the rattlesnakes handled by hillbillies in a state of religious exaltation."[4]

In his *Ivory Towers and Sacred Founts: The Artist as Hero in Fiction from Goethe to Joyce* (1964), Maurice Beebe asserts that a longstanding conflict between opposing ideals - the Ivory Tower and the Sacred Fount - should be the focus of a study of novels about artists:

> The former insists that the true artist must hold himself aloof from life, while the latter finds the source of art in experience. The artist is pulled in both directions simultaneously because his needs as a human being are not those of his creative self. Almost always the two selves are at odds, and it is a rarely fortunate artist who achieves happiness and success both as a man and creator. Yet the artist who moves too far in either direction and separates art from life is more likely to fail than the artist who attains a balance between his two selves.[5]

Beebe maintains that good writers like Balzac, Proust, James and Joyce (or rather their artist-heroes) manage to balance these opposing claims and "resolve the conflict between the outside world and their internal vision." They show that "it is possible to move back and forth between the Tower and the Fount." Yet they also "have a common insistence" (Beebe is faced with a contradiction) that "the artist *as artist* must turn his back on life."

Stopping with Joyce, Beebe feels that portrayals of the artist in fiction after *A Portrait of the Artist as a Young Man* (1916) seem "to follow the tradition already established without changing it in any important way."[6] This generalization does not hold. The writer-novels of the postwar decades, even in the 1950s, radically depart from Joyce because the heroes typically perceive neither worldly experience as a primal source of wisdom, nor aloofness as a fountain of inspiration. Also, and more importantly, they do not aim at internal equilibrium and order because they no longer hold that it is the writer's responsibility to balance art and life. Instead, they search for ways of integrating or interplaying the two. Functioning with equal eloquence in the metafictional vein and in the older realistic modes, blending the two, they flaunt a passion for re-defining their profession's energies and attitudes - not for equilibrium.

Lee T. Lemon contends, in *Portraits of the Artist in Contemporary Fiction* (1985), that fictional portraits of artists since James Joyce have changed notably, especially after World War II, because they have shifted from what Lemon calls the "Byronic mold" to the "Wordsworthian" one, that is, from visions of "isolated rebels" filled with contempt for the ordinary world, to those of the common lot, in fact "anti-artists" who try to live like others.[7] Lemon's dictum has limited application in discussing recent American fiction.[*] Writer-heroes may have lost, or given up, much of their age-long conviction that they function as society's spiritual priests, the moral center of their culture, but they now demonstrate a new sense of self-assurance and distance. They like to see themselves as operators of human imagination, as jugglers of the confessional mode, as magicians in the funhouse of verbal possibilities. They embrace alternate histories of their culture, portray themselves imaginatively, insist on disrupting old attitudes while simultaneously devising new

---

[*]John Barth is the only American author discussed by Lemon.

ones. All this places them as far away from ordinary men and women as they had been in the past.

These fictional identities are frequently elusive, their attitudes subjective to the extreme, their aims and freedoms projected, then questioned, ridiculed or even rejected. Like the archetypal trickster, they lay traps, confuse, play games. Treating fiction as a medium uniquely renewable, a mode of infinite transformations that produces, paradoxically, a sense of authenticity, these writer-heroes evade formulaic definitions and transcend paradigms. Indeed, they undermine potential interpretation, or criticism of the structures within which they operate. They obsessively demonstrate that American reality is a matter of illusion, that themes and literature in general are about matters other than themselves, that events and lives are characterized by endless dimensions and infinite reflections - decentered and unfixed.

Fiction's postwar writer-heroes commonly practice contradictions and employ heterogenous world views. Working from the center of paradox they implement lifestyles, themes, or metaphors which they declare unavailable or radically unacceptable. They claim, for example, they are unable to create, yet come forward with successful works. They deplore cultural depravity and deterioration, yet they are inspired by them. They complain there is no appreciative and sincere audience, yet long for and often gain market success. They distort images of themselves for the purpose of thwarting reader expectations, then say such exposure is painful. However, in containing such opposing, fragmented features, they manage to defend themselves from aimlessness, paralysis, or formlessness which, critics like Tony Tanner argue, characteristically beset the American hero.[*]

My aim in this book has been to bring together a substantial number of works of literature published in the United States in the second half of the 20th century in which protagonists are involved in writing in a manner that is more or less

---

[*]In *City of Words* (1971), Tanner sees the central American character, frequently a writer, as caught between a need to "find a freedom which is not a jelly," and establishing an identity "which is not a prison." [Tony Tanner, *City of Words* (New York: Harper and Row, 1971), pp. 19-20.]

functional, and to sketch on the basis of it an overview of existing tendencies, attitudes and occurrences, to create a composite sketch of the writer-hero of the second half of the century.

As any register of a genre must be, my study is necessarily selective. I refer to texts which can be broadly called fiction, or prose, or novels. These have become ambiguous terms today. Penetrated with journalism, autobiography, memoirs, letters, reportage, they stress interchangeability of experience, fragmentation, paradox, irony, parody. Autobiographical confessions focus on "real writer's" emotions and imaginative constructs rather than on his person or history. Real-life authors enter their narratives only to distort the factual and/or to obscure ontological boundaries. "All my works are indeed chapters from my personal experience," says a writer character in Philip Roth's *Operation Shylock*, "but nevertheless they are not 'the story of my life.'" He then adds with characteristic postmodernist irony: "The things that are most true are easily falsified."[8]

I do not attempt to balance existing genres, or to show writers in a multiracial framework, or to inflate voids. The female writer-heroine, for example, remains characteristically underrepresented in postwar American fiction. Feminism has not yet offered portraits of women ready to explore the relationship between themselves as artists and contemporary problems, or between gender and effective literary expression. Writing for them still functions as a weapon in their struggle against stereotypes and inequality, as opposed to using fiction as a forum for innovative stylistic devices, or to rework historical-literary concerns, which are examined, for example, in Bellow's *Humboldt's Gift*.

The structure of this study, although implicitly chronological, is above all thematic. The Introduction focuses on how the novels of the 1950s and early 1960s reflect, comically and absurdly, a sense of exhaustion and depravity, mental numbness and emptiness. Writer-protagonists project themselves as murky and haunted selves determined by exterior chaos and complemented by interior anxiety, as unaccomplished artisans involved in futile attempts to seek renewal.

Chapter One deals with the new wave of expression freed by meta- and self-reflexive fiction in the 1960s and later decades. Absorbed by the reflection of fiction itself as technique, writer-heroes discover that confusion and loss may be a way of reclaiming art. They boldly discard older patterns of literary representation, invent verbal labyrinths from which they insist they cannot escape, establish new relationships with other characters, and discover new means of linking the mimetic with the metafictional.

Confronting everyday existence, writers in fiction often vacillate between exuberance and anxiety. Many speak of being lonely and loveless, isolated and withdrawn. In Chapter Two I look at these and other aspects of their confrontation with American experience. Though accusatory, heroes are frequently inspired, or energized, by moral corruption, violence, terrorism or conspiracy. Their views of city life and relationships with women are similarly contradictory. Their perspectives on Europe are an arresting mixture of horror and fascination, puzzlement and confusion.

In Chapter Three I look at writers' intellectual, creative and professional concerns. Largely critical of their cultural pedigree, or other writers' views, they concentrate on the challenges and frustrations of a writer ensnared by materialism and media glitz. However, underneath such complaints lies another interesting contradiction. Today's writer-heroes gladly substitute the time-honored tradition of the artist's resistance to fame and wealth for a desire for market success and popularity. These, when they come, bring various forms of backlash, which writers in turns lament and obsessively analyze.

ACKNOWLEDGEMENTS

Throughout the work on this book many people provided me with help, advice and encouragement. I am indebted to Prof. Agnieszka Salska and Prof. Jerzy Poradecki of Łódź University, to Professors David Kesterson, Lee Miller and Bob Stevens of the University of North Texas, to Prof. Helen Gościlo of the University of Pittsburgh, to Prof. Michel Granger of the University of Lyon and Prof. David Pichasky of the University of Minnesota. I am particularly grateful to Prof. Clifford Hallam, visiting lecturer in Łódź, for reading my manuscript and offering wise comments and suggestions for its improvement. I also wish to thank Łódź University for providing me with grants and friendly encouragement.

GENERAL INTRODUCTION

THE YEARS OF ANXIETY

DANGLING IN CHAOS

Paradoxically, America's emergence from World War II as a military, political and economic world power brings in its wake an intense and widespread sense of defeat among the country's intellectuals and artists. Their confusion and inertia are different from the "fatigued suspension of the will" following WWI that resulted in an inquiry into the thematic and formal possibilities of literature.[9] After the Second World War, young American writers express disillusionment rather than rebellion, and often defer to the conservative sensibilities of the previous era. "The intellectuals, far from thinking of themselves as a desperate 'opposition,'...have all, even the handful who still try to retain a glower of criticism, become responsible and moderate. And tame," observes Irving Howe in 1952.[10]

By the early 1950s, economic prosperity and rampant consumerism create a mood of optimism which becomes the semi-official, politically correct attitude throughout the entire decade and beyond. The literary artist who refuses to conform is socially and politically suspect. Critics and commentators accuse writers of failing their medium, of producing irrelevant, obscurantist and derivative work. Some insist that pessimism is temporary, a cyclic pattern of cultural waywardness, a passing vogue of failure. Van Wyck Brooks contends that postwar American literature reflects, not so much a disintegration of the outside world, but rather a surrender to "the spiritual climate of our time," a kind of fashionable and obligatory "reversion to barbarism." He urges American writers to "break the evil spell that weighs upon their minds" and find ways of rehumanizing literature and stimulating a faith in human goodness.[11]

But the prevailing mood of entrapment, alienation and futility persists; it takes root and blooms in a ruined garden of uncertainty - a mode of gloom and radical irony that will mold American literature for decades to come. Some critics recognize a major cultural dislocation, a permanently changed condition of the postwar mind. John W. Aldridge points out that after the Second World War it is no longer possible to write novels because writers confront a society uniquely lacking in traditional, deep-seated values. "The best young writers of the second war and its aftermath," he writes in his influential *After the Lost Generation* (1951), "have come to maturity at the end of the period of transition and loss when the wreckage of the old order has been made complete and the energy of rebellion has been dissipated."[12] Malcolm Cowley acknowledges that "the new novelists have a special reason for their feelings of deprivation" because they have lost not only their faith in progress, but also "the old American conviction that most people are good and that evil is merely an accident."[13] Irving Howe fears that the spirit of modernism now coming to an end is being replaced by a literature geared toward a modern "half welfare, half-garrison society" whose writers can express only "the hovering sickness of soul, the despairing contentment, the prosperous malaise."[14] Edmund Fuller, Ihab Hassan, and Marcus Klein similarly document the fallen state of the American literary hero, his aimlessness and his refusal to accept the absurd contradictions of postwar America.

Leslie Fiedler sees mainstream American fiction from Cooper to Hemingway as an expression of adolescent fantasy: the wish to escape the restrictions of civilization and the responsibilities of family by "lighting out for the territory," often with a non-white companion. These adventures with homo-erotic implications are seen as a displaced indictment of the guilt-ridden American male, "the man on the run" who never grew up.[*]

---

[*]Regarding Fiedler's speculations, John W. Aldridge argues that Fiedler is "as much a romantic as those whom he condemns" and, in fact, himself betrays the confusion and despondency of the postwar author. "Deep down in his heart he hates himself for not being a writer," says Aldridge. Several years later, Fiedler published *The Second Stone* (1963), a novel that became something of a literary event because of Fiedler's reputation. It reflects patterns typical for the early postwar writer-

Sociologist David Riesman points out, in *The Lonely Crowd* (1953),* that in the fast-changing American society the new, "other-directed" man has a need to conform and that the nascent consumer-oriented, urbanized patterns undercut his individuality and destroy creativity. Riesman speculates that, in the hands of the contemporary writer, the new hero will drive the novel to extinction, or to the discovery of new dramatic effects.

W.H. Auden's 1947 poem "The Age of Anxiety," set in New York during the war, establishes the cultural shibboleth for American postwar literary disenchantment. But Auden, an intelligent and sympathetic observer, implies that anxiety, a relatively new feature of American culture, contains intriguing and possibly fertile contradictions. Literary heroes' new passivity, their lack of "honor and history," their frequently confessed paucity of free will and moral responsibility, Auden contends, clash with America's reputation as "the freest on earth." The medium that contains them - the novel - comprises another, "common and unnoticed," incongruity. Endowed by the very nature of the literary craft with the freedom to project virtually unconstrained visions of life, fiction increasingly proposes situations in which characters are incapable of choice, "the absolute victim(s) of circumstance."[15] Two decades later the incongruities of which Auden speaks are seen as sources of the novel's vitality as well as the hero's energy and inspiration. Meanwhile, however, writer-heroes that emerge in American fiction declare themselves numbed, vacuous, paralyzed. They are overwhelmed by frustration and anger, guilt-ridden, lacking faith in responsibility and moral order. Their conduct is joyless, uneasy, defensive. Saul Bellow's *Dangling Man* (1944)

---

hero. Clem Stone, an American writer living in Rome in the Fifties, fails to write a novel of his war experiences, and turns from a young angry rebel into a middle-aged poseur. [John Aldridge, *In Search of Heresy: American Literature in an Age of Conformity* (New York: McGraw-Hill, 1956, p.41.]

*For similar observations of the period, see William H. Whyte's *The Organization Man* (1955).

offers a fitting metaphor for such qualities.* But dangling as an image of a cultural-psychological crisis is not new to American fiction. Henry Miller uses it to describe the plight of modern man in *Tropic of Cancer* (1934), a brazen and passionate landmark of the American need to declare the new tone of pessimism. Its writer-narrator lashes bitterly at "the Great Western civilization":

> Are these men and women, I ask myself, or are these shadows, shadows of puppets dangled by invisible strings? They move in freedom apparently, but they have nowhere to go.[16]

Later, in *Nights of Love and Laughter* (1955), the demonic figure of a scarred and misshapen war veteran turned writer thus defines the generation stigmatized by war and the resulting sense of loss:

> We're the lost legion of the defeated archangels. We're dangling in chaos and our leaders, blinder than bats, bray like jackasses.[17]

The story's narrator, Miller's persona, shares the veteran's revulsion, yet comes to doubt his integrity. He reproaches the man for letting himself be used, in the past, by corrupt ideologies, for withdrawing from society, for distorting his story and making "a vice of...suffering" in order to rouse his listeners' sympathy.[18]

A number of novels of the 1940s and 1950s explore what the Miller persona scorns - self-dramatized personal anguish and suffering. Joseph, the youthful protagonist in *Dangling Man*, pronounces himself painfully lost and alienated amid the trauma and changes of wartime America. He feels bereft of personal choice and moral certainties, a victim of "a condemned age" no longer guided by God and

---

*Modifying this image for the space-conscious 1960s and 1970s, Frederick Karl sees these decades as similarly belonging to "comic tragedians...dangling...outside a spaceship." "Comparably, our literary heroes in the sixties and seventies are those who left the world behind, a notable distance from the nineteenth-century creature for whom Emerson said "Life only avails." [Frederick Karl, *American Fictions 1940-1980* (New York: Harper and Row, 1983), p. 29.]

consequently overwhelmed by the blind mechanical rule of society. Though not a novelist, or even a writer as such, he simply records fragments of his broodings and uses his erratic daily "acts of the imagination" as a source of spiritual sustenance and a measure of identity. He is too aimless and disoriented to see his life as material for art, or art as an escape from life in suspension.

Clarence Feiler of "The Gonzaga Manuscripts" (1954)[*], another early Bellow character, though no longer guided by the dark defeatism which overwhelms Joseph, functions in a parallel manner. This young American, "lanky and pained," with no occupation and "nothing to do," envisions literature as a means of salvation.[19] Like his fictional peers, he is skeptical about the value of the existing literary legacy. Modern literature, he muses, "this sort of grand council considering what mankind should do next," is not doing people "much good." Writers and poets have been "fixing values," or trying "to supply a substitute" at the time when "God doesn't rule over men as he used to."[20] He finds some hope and inspiration by studying the Spanish poet, Manuel Gonzaga, whose manuscripts he tries to salvage in Fascist Spain. Gonzaga is unique:

> ...a human being who spoke only as a human being; there was nothing spurious about him. He tried never to misrepresent; he wanted to see. To move you he didn't have to do anything, he merely had to be. We've made the most natural things the hardest of all.[21]

Clarence strives to recover an Eden of literary sensitivity. But his stay in Spain brings a sense of futility instead of renewal. He never manages to rescue his idol's manuscripts, or to learn more about his life. He is disillusioned; his attempts to bring mankind much-needed spiritual guidance are ignored or mocked, a "punishment." "Numb and motionless," he leaves Spain.[22]

Early postwar writer-protagonists inhabit the narrow territory between the

---

[*]Later included in *Mosby's Memoirs and Other Stories* (1968).

dull defeatism of *Dangling Man* and the radical innocence of the naive youth in "The Gonzaga Manuscripts." Mikey Lovett, in Norman Mailer's *Barbary Shore* (1951), plans to write "a large and ambitious work" about the state of his country, but hampered by amnesia, a condition caused by the war, he is unable to reconstruct his own past, or his identity. The room in the boarding house in which he lives is subleased to him, symbolically, by an author known for "superficial optimism," one who "like so many writers...had very little interest in people."[23] The house resounds with the endless ideological quarrels of its inhabitants. Their beliefs, radical and bizarre, darkly complicated by conspiracies, by sex and violence, are dangerous, Lovett feels, threatening to return mankind to "barbary." Disoriented, depressed and spiritually exhausted, unable to write, Lovett flees the house of conflict under cover of night. He withdraws into his imagination, to him a more secure reality. Here, "time passes, and I work and I study, and I keep my eye on the door."[24] *

Mailer's other novel of the fifties, *The Deer Park* (1955), features a similarly apathetic and confused writer-protagonist. Sergius O'Shaugnessy is a young man who sees his own past as both useless and tormenting, a terrible emptiness created largely by his uncertain parentage, early orphanhood, and painful memories of his military service as a fighter pilot in Korea. While languishing at Desert D'Or, the fabled resort community for the Hollywood elite, he is unable to focus, to resist illusion:

> ...I hardly wrote a word while I was at the resort....I do not know if I can
> explain that I did not want to feel too much, and I did not want to think. I had
> the idea that there were two worlds. There was a real world as I called it, a
> world of wars and boxing clubs and children's homes on back streets, and

---

*The paradox addressed by Auden is characteristic of Lovett, a man disaffiliated from the past, confused by the "rotten" present, recoiled into self-imposed isolation and loneliness. As a failed writer he is the antithesis of Mailer, who entered the literary scene after *The Naked and the Dead* (1948) and established himself as a well-known media figure, a lavishly self-advertized novelist, as well as public persona involved in brilliant and controversial arguments concerning the country's political and cultural tensions.

this real world was a world where orphans burned orphans. It was better not even to think of this. I liked the other world in which almost everybody lived. The imaginary world.[25]

As he attempts to express himself in writing, to find a style, to verbalize his rage, Sergius thinks of Hemingway, the 1950s symbol of artistic self-assurance based on personal experience. But his attempt to live and write like Hemingway fails and he comes to realize that "it is not creatively satisfying to repeat the work of a good writer."[26] Besides, he feels Hemingway himself could not have coped artistically with the illusory world of Desert D'Or. To describe self-deception by using the novelist's inventiveness, Sergius fears, reduces one to "a galley-slave to his imagination."[27] At the end of the novel, having refused a handsome sum for the rights to his life story, he leaves Desert D'Or, travels in Mexico and eventually settles in Greenwich Village. Here, as the novel ends, he reads and writes, tries to acquire "the most elusive habit of all, the mind of the writer."[28] *

Some of the anxieties which Sergius experiences but fails to rework into art are better demarcated in Mailer's "The Man Who Studied Yoga" (1952), yet another Mailer story (which he calls a short novel) about the postwar novelist's disorientation and mental stupor. The principal character, Sam Slovoda dreams of becoming a serious author, "of consequence in the world," but has actually never written anything.[29] His confusing and distracting life has drained him of creative energy. His lament is familiar. Like Harry in Hemingway's "The Snows of Kilimanjaro," Sam

---

*In *Advertisements for Myself*, Mailer admits he changed the original text after the novel had been sent to the publisher (who reneged on the contract). "Now, after three years of living with the book, I could at last admit the style was wrong, that it had been wrong from the time I started it, that I had been strangling the life of my novel in a poetic prose which was too self-consciously attractive and formal, false to the life of my characters, especially false to the life of my narrator who was the voice of my novel...." By changing the style of *The Deer Park*, making it "rough," giving its voice "an abrupt and muscular body," Mailer feels he equips Sergius, previously an "overdelicate, oversensitive, and painfully tender" young man with confidence and courage, qualities which he finds ultimately self-punishing and self-violating. "I was now creating a man who was braver and stronger than me, and the more my new style succeeded, the more was I writing an implicit portrait of myself as well." [*Advertisements for Myself* (New York: Putnam, 1959), pp.235-238.]

confronts loneliness and defeat, loathes his associates, and blames his wife for his failure. Yet Sam and Harry reveal terrors that clearly belong to different psychological and artistic orientations. To Harry, the aspiring writer of the 1920s and 1930s, life is emotionally disorganized and mentally distracting, yet tenable in its ordered morality and traditional perception of experience. Harry knows that his own weakness has largely emptied his life. To Sam, a former Communist, now a confused "rebel," the reality of the 1950s is strangely and painfully disjointed and irrelevant, a "schizoid" decade he is not able to transmute into form and subject matter, partly because the language, Sam feels, has become exhausted and abused, "doomed to the fashion of the moment."[30] If Harry is a case of artistic self-betrayal, Sam stands for aesthetic burnout and terminal confusion.

> The novelist, thinks Sam, perspiring beneath blankets, must live in paranoia and seek to be one with the world; he must be terrified of experience and hungry for it; he must think himself nothing and believe he is superior to all. The feminine in his nature cries for proof he is a man; he dreams of power and is without capacity to gain it; he loves himself above all and therefore despises all that he is.[31]

Sam knows that realism is a poor literary vehicle because "reality" is no longer available to a novelist, it is "no longer realistic."[32] He is mortified by the fact that he cannot conceive of a convincing hero. An ideal hero for our times, he calculates, should be "a man of action and contemplation, capable of sin, large enough for good, a man immense," someone who "reasonably could not exist."[33]

When Mailer was bringing his tormented protagonists to life, he measured himself against Hemingway, the accepted model of discipline and artistic confidence. Yet, from 1946 to his death in 1961, Hemingway himself labored in anguish and radical uncertainty to portray a disconcerted, baffled writer-hero - the author's hidden self. In the event, the immense, disorganized manuscript was not published until 1986 as *The Garden of Eden*, a problematical text featuring David

Bourne, a young successful writer who sees life as menacing, intangible and morally bankrupt.* His newly married wife, Catherine, engages in perverse sexual antics and deeply resents his devotion to literature. His own flagging faith in his ability to use experience as a source of artistic reflection, his recurring uneasiness about the world, and his perceived vulnerability frighten him. He recognizes in himself a growing need to withdraw from life's "overpopulated vacancy of madness" and to take refuge in an inner niche of idealized visions, the blissful "country of the story."[34]

Vestiges of the Hemingway hero's artistic self-assurance occur in *The Garden of Eden*. His well-known creed that the artist must have the strength to assert control over life, to protect his inner core is, at the end, reiterated by the hero. David assures himself that life can be controlled, that once creative work is under way anxiety dissipates. He triumphs in the realization that he has managed to write an even better version of the story Catherine destroyed. Yet moments of frightening weakness are revealed. The conflict between the public, mythic, confident Hemingway, and his inner, more complex vision of an artist is disclosed.** For the first time a Hemingway hero confesses that he "tried not to think but talked and listened in the unreality that reality had become."[35]

Younger writers, often not yet accomplished, or unprotected by status and popularity, and unable to contain their distress, are typically less cryptic about the pressures of the postwar years. During the 1950s and the early 1960s a number of novels emerge featuring writers that speak of unfulfilled ambitions and aborted

---

*E.L.Doctorow asserts that judging by the inventory of the writer's manuscripts, "Hemingway intended *The Garden of Eden* as a major work." He believes that the novel's very title "suggests a governing theme of his [Hemingway's] life." ["Braver Than We Thought," *The New York Times Book Review*, May 18, 1986.]

**Malcolm O. Magaw postulates that *The Garden of Eden* is the "final portrait of the artist as a young man and hero...a composite of the Adam before the Fall and the Adam after the Fall," the man who knows the new anguish but tries to be strong enough to endure it. It is more likely that, overwhelmed by anxiety and confusion, the aging novelist was unable to express a coherent view of his disintegrating world, and that he did not want to see his earlier myth being verified. We know for certain that, unable to make the massive manuscript convincing, or even manageable, he decided against publication. [Malcolm O. Magaw, "The Fusion of History and Immediacy: Hemingway's Artist-Hero in *The Garden of Eden*," *CLIO, A Journal of Literature, History and the Philosophy of History*, Vol.17, #1, Fall 1987.]

careers, of art that becomes truncated, of themes that prove elusive or too intimidating for the author's sensitivity. The autobiographical elements appear starkly urgent but painfully unreworked. Heroes speak of the frantic struggle for sanity and self-preservation; they are burdened by fear and guilt. Some of their complaints are lengthy and sustained. Others are brief and indirect. Characters merely suggest their putative identity as writers. They emerge as potential rather than productive authors. For example, Holden Caulfield, in Salinger's *The Catcher in the Rye* (1951), hospitalized for a mental breakdown, discloses only in passing that the story of his confusing and distressing New York episode is a therapeutic exercise, a narrative by which he hopes to reconstruct himself, to regain the world's consent to function within its "phony" covenants. The narrator of Ellison's *Invisible Man* (1952) assumes he can write about his experiences; then, numbed in his underground retreat, he decides to burn his manuscript, to him evidence of obsolete identities and useless endeavors. Esther Greenwood, in Sylvia Plath's *The Bell Jar* (1963), aspires to write about herself, an effort which, though carried out "only in disguise," may provide her with a way of asserting her personality, give her a sense of identity and fulfillment. The task is not accomplished. She realizes she is a creature under a "glass bell jar, stewing in my own sour air," whose paralyzing depression deprives her of the capacity to write about herself, or her times.[36] She survives several suicide attempts but never manages to function satisfactorily - or to incorporate her experience in writing.

MANIC-DEPRESSION AND THE COUNTERCULTURE HERO

Writer-protagonists who emerge out of the Beat culture of the 1950s are better at expressing visions of freedom, or at demonstrating their defiance, than at acting as the movement's artistic observers eager to capture in writing its aesthetics, or to refer it to larger social and cultural issues of their times. Interested in their own responses to acts of rebellion, the Beat heroes do not perceive themselves as functioning agents of a literary breakthrough, even when they claim they are writers of a new awareness.

The hero of Jack Kerouac's *On the Road* (1957) is the prototypical case in point. Sal Paradise - the irony of the name symbolism is multivalent - ricochets from coast to coast mixing with junkies, hoboes, prophets and misfits, all the "mad drunken Americans in the mighty land," yet soon realizes that irresponsible flight patterns do not achieve deliverance or lasting inspiration. Tedium, restlessness and a sense of void await at the end of each frantic cross-country ride. A life-style attuned to sensation, to temporary highs or kicks, fails to compensate for feckless ideas. "We were on the roof of America and all we could do was yell, I guess - across the night, eastward over the Plains," muses Sal while viewing the spacious grandeur of a Western landscape, and this observation captures his conviction that adolescent joy rides are shallow and inconsequential. He is similarly aware that life on the road virtually negates serious writing because, beneath the fever of drugs, hasty sex and occasional jazz, he discovers no authentic need, or ability, to understand man's relation to the world passing by at 60 mph. Dean Moriarty, always enthusiastic, urges him to record their life on the road ("Man, wow, there's so many things to do, so many things to write!"); yet Sal's novel does not treat on-the-road ecstasy, but presents "some gloomy tale of New York" aimed to satisfy "a Hollywood director" - hackwork for money.[37]

In *Dharma Bums* (1958), where mountain hiking replaces frenetic cross-country joyrides, and derivative Zen Buddhism supercedes the vague "Hemingway imitation" Sal assumes in *On the Road*, young men hope to find themselves through poetry, voluntary poverty, free love and separation from society.[38] Japhy Ryder, a young poet resembling Gary Snyder[*], dreams of a "great rucksack revolution" in which "thousands or even millions" of young Americans are voluntarily converted into "Zen lunatics," pilgrims of new American innocence and joy.[39] He hopes his

---

[*]Other characters also closely resemble real-life Beats: Ray Smith is Kerouac's alter ego, Alvah Goldbook, author of "Wail," is an obvious guise for Allen Ginsberg.

own long poem called "Rivers and Mountains Without End," a construction "like a river, or like one of them real long Chinese silk paintings" will provide him with a sense of creative eternity, a chance to spend "three thousand years writing it."[40] Japhy's and his friends' escapism achieve fresh and lyrical quality not found in *On the Road*; the intimacy with nature is deeply reflective and more sensuous. But the ideas remain false and sentimental, a youthful masquerade disguising the basic inability to address postwar America.

Likewise, a mood of aimlessness infuses *The Subterraneans* (1958), a novel in which the Beat mixture of vitality and alienation is given inward, more candidly sexual, even somewhat intellectual, dramatizations. Leo Percepied, a writer who perceives himself as a bum, an egomaniac and a drug-addict - as well as a new Baudelaire - recounts his brief and haunting love affair with a black girl, Mardou Fox. His "wanting to be vital, alive like a Negro or an Indian" mingles with exalted sufferings of lost love, along with a concern for a literary heritage that has become disrupted:

> ...ah me Hart Crane Melville and all ye assorted brother poets of the American night that once I thought would be my sacrificial altar and now it is but who's to care, know, and I lost love because of it - drunkard, dullard, poet....[41]

The book is filled with a sense of belatedness, as well as bitterness that the Beat mission, conceived in ideal terms, has become corrupt and dissipated. Enthusiasm is replaced by a fear of losing vitality, of disorientation. The hero declares, ruefully, in the opening lines that

> Once I was young and had so much more orientation and could talk with nervous intelligence about everything and with clarity and without as much literary preambling as this; in other words this is the story of an unself-confident man....[42]

John Clellon Holmes's *Go* (1952), an important early Beat novel that preceded *On the Road*, to which it is often compared, reads like an alternative, more cerebral version of the latter. The familiar cast of thinly-disguised principal actors of the Beat movement troop through the narrative. Kerouac is called Gene Pasternak, Ginsberg becomes David Stofsky. Hart Kennedy, with his Cadillac, is a more sedate, but flatter, version of Neal Cassady, Kerouac's Dean Moriarty. They scurry tirelessly from bar to bar, party to party hunting for marijuana, listen to jazz, engage in brief erotic flings, talk of living things out - all in an attempt to discover the psychic frontiers of "a new season."[43] But their hunger for spiritual renewal again has a built-in fear of the void, of creative energies being spent. Stofsky, who has lost trust in knowledge, including psychotherapy, feels there is "a monster" everywhere in life, "our whole horrible, ego filled world, sick! The spirit sick! 'O rose, thou art sick!'"[44] He yearns for simple childlike feelings, and turns to Blake for a healing mystic vision.

The writer called Paul Hobbes, an intelligent but disillusioned Marxist and war veteran, whose marriage has become bland and "oddly centerless," reflects on the fragility of his rebellious friends, their "half humorous, half mystical ideas, mortared with bits of poetry and insights derived from religious paintings."[45] He understands their rancor, but deplores their moral and intellectual limitations, the triviality of their lifestyle; Hobbes (symbolizing the lonely and brutish life without society) foresees the coming of a cultural mental despondency, a "depression...thick and centerless."[46] He himself is torn between a desire to share in the exuberant search for freedom, and life that is based on order and tradition. Not satisfied with the book he has completed, he loses interest. Like his fellow Beats, Pasternak or Stofsky, like most writing heroes of the 1950s, he reveals little about his writing or how it relates to his life.

Ken Kesey, inspired by the Beat luminaries, especially Neal Cassady, becomes in the early 1960s a public embodiment of the movement's patterns of enthusiasm, dissension and rejection. Having achieved significant critical praise and popular acclaim with *One Flew Over the Cuckoo's Nest* (1962), he temporarily abandons writing and assumes leadership of a bizarre and unconventional group called The Merry Pranksters, whose experiments with drugs, travels across the country in an old school bus painted psychedelic, and a penchant for various audio-visual games and presentations serve as a beacon to the growing hippie culture. The Prankster ethos, the harbinger of the sexual-drug revolution of the decades to come, is captured by Tom Wolfe in *The Electric Kool-Aid Acid Test* (1968), an early nonfiction novel. Kesey's "strange up-country charisma" and his "vital energy" help create the Pranksters' "most fantastic experiment in human consciousness," a mission aiming to proselytize the society, convert it to the freedom of psychedelic experience.[47]

A novelist turned guru, the Kesey character views writing as "an old-fashioned and artificial form." He prefers to live out the energies and needs of his time directly, to become an agent of liberation and spiritual potency, a high priest of "things common to Hindus, Buddhists, Christians, and for that matter Theosophists and even flying-saucer cultists."[48] But he discovers that his new role proves finally vacuous because the country is increasingly aimless, self-consuming, cancerous. The attempt to attend the Beatles concert evokes an image of beastly menace looming over the young people of the nation:

> CANCER - Kesey has only to look and it is perfectly obvious - all of them, the teeny freaks and the Beatles, are one creature, caught in a state of sheer poison mad cancer. The Beatles are the creature's head. The teeny freaks are the body. But the head has lost control of the body and the body rebels and goes amok and that is what cancer is. The vibrations of it hit the Pranksters, in a clump, stoned out of their gourds, in sickening ways.[49]

Deeply concerned about these dark forces, dismayed by the Pranksters' inability to fully articulate, or to achieve creative mastery, realizing his followers are too dependent upon him, Kesey anticipates the breakup of the commune. This indeed occurs when, after fleeing to Mexico, he returns to serve a short sentence for marijuana possession. When released, he settles on a farm in Oregon and begins "working on a novel."[50]

In more recent fiction, Kesey frequently views his public odyssey with the same sadness and dismay underlying the novels of Kerouac and Holmes. In *Demon Box* (1986), Devlin Deboree, Kesey's persona, admits that the experiment and quest, the whole "revolution" of the sixties may have been largely lost. He deplores the general decline of values, the misuse of drugs, the growth of violence, and he grieves over the death of icons such as Neal Cassady and John Lennon. More recently, in *The Further Inquiry* (1990), Kesey envisages the Pranksters defending themselves in a mock trial. Called to testify, he confesses to the damage done, but also claims that the Pranksters helped America exorcise the stifling postwar puritanism of the 1950s.

As in the fiction of Kerouac and other Beat writers, William Burroughs' work, an impressive oeuvre spanning four decades, is also suffused with the restless search for volatile, aimless action, for male adventure (often explicitly homosexual), for hallucinogenic bliss. His novels are informed by nervous, erratic, sometimes extraterrestrial, movements from place to place, from one high to another. But their decor and plots are highly eccentric and ostentatious, a grotesque admixture of pornography and science-fiction. People are casually tortured, orgasms are chromatic revelations, fires flash from fundaments, otherworldly creatures invade our civilization. Drugs, which to the Beats are a promise of a more amiable and ecstatic world are, to Burroughs, a deadly force, an inescapable, never ending source of entrapment and terror.

The Burroughs persona is source of an oddly uncomplicated and repetitious presence that echoes Burroughs himself because it contains fragments of the writer's biography and his various obsessions: drugs, the occult, explicit homosexual fantasies and practices. *Naked Lunch* (1959), a text steeped in the surrealistic and hallucinatory, the disjointed and the violent, features a familiar voice, recognizable but grotesquely warped, that offers cynical and grimly humorous rejection of conventional moral choices, or acceptable social functions. It is a haunted presence that simultaneously contains and escapes itself.

Burroughs renounces the coherent narrator, or fixed patterns of language, thematic principles, or consistent versions of reality because underlying everything is addiction; moreover, his novelistic persona, though clearly a fictional agent, refuses to assume the role of a fiction-maker. Words and thought patterns in their traditional form are seen as a destructive scheme imposed upon mankind, a "virus," or a cosmic force infecting every region of terrestrial life, including language. "...Burroughs is really writing about all the different ways human identity is devoured in the modern world, how the self is dissolved or pre-empted by nameless forces radically antipathetic to the human image," observes Tony Tanner, and the remark describes well the Burroughs persona in *Naked Lunch*.[51] But there is a paradox here. Burroughs suggests that writing is also a safeguard against life's terror and annihilation. Trying to rid oneself of the conditioning enslavement of words, the undeclared writer in his fiction creates a consciousness that is a work of art in itself. It is a presence endowed with literary significance, a construct whose psychic survival depends on writing out one's inner struggle and chaos. Freed of dependence on life's norms and habits, the trap of oneself, of one's language, it needs to return, through fiction, to the congruity of literary creation, to a truth hidden in formless, meandering, collaged art.

Kim Lee, a Burroughs-like character in *Queer* (1985), does not realize that his literary awareness exists on some deeper level of his intuition, as Burroughs explains in the introduction to the novel:

> Lee does not know that he is already committed to writing, since this is the only way he has of making an indelible record, whether Allerton is inclined to observe or not. Lee is being inexorably pressed into the world of fiction. He has already made the choice between his life and his work.[52]

Though the Burroughs persona foregrounds alienation, the power of drugs and the occult, as well as various expressions of anti-social behavior in ways that writers like Holmes, Kerouac, or Mailer never attempted, he remains a tormented loner on the move across the coarse and violent landscapes of the modern world, a frenzied Quixote in search of some ultimate solution to man's disgust with civilization. He does not escape his enemies because they are internal, and his missions lead him nowhere. His fears of being subjugated or exploited by the cancerous presence of universal bureaucracy and the many repressive forces of modern life remain. He creates new conflicts as he moves on, inflicts pain on others as well himself; he obsessively pursues pleasure but never achieves lasting satisfaction.

Unlike the other Beats, Burroughs does not celebrate the writer's suffering, or lament his flight.[*] In fact, by going beyond existing moral standards, he attempts to find an expanded perception, a viable system in which human insubordination does not conflict with conventional social or cultural patterns. His novelistic personae yearn for escape into some free, unobstructed, pure territory where life and art are unadulterated, even by fictional devices.

REALITY AS FRAUD, OR SICKNESS

An émigré writer of European sensibilities and background, Vladimir Nabokov, like Burroughs, creates a distinctive and characteristically extreme reflection of repression and vitality in the 1950s. His heroes are loners, creatures of conscious isolation who express contempt for the commonplace of human life and thought. They interpret the world freely, act out subversion, fixations, or sexual obsessions. Quite consciously, they complement moral perversion with stylistic experimentation. In the case of Burroughs, characters are bent on destroying the structure of language. Their use of repetition, quotation and cut-up texts aims at the

---

[*] Burroughs' obsessive devotion to experiments in violence and chronic, self-destructive behavior does not (most likely because of extraordinary luck or genetic endowment) lead to his own untimely death, as in the case of Ernest Hemingway, Malcolm Lowry, Sylvia Plath, Jerzy Kosinski, et al.

disruption of the traditional meaning and hegemony of language, of the reading experience itself. Nabokov's heroes, by contrast, expand endlessly the possibilities of the individual consciousness through verbal play, highly-imaginative games, tricks, riddles, self-created and self-perpetuating absurdities. They assume that life is an artistic arrangement which can be appropriated and reworked at will, that it is most interesting when it goes beyond stylistic conventions and accepted moral standards.

Trying to live out such views, however, is never easy for Nabokov's protagonists, a number of whom are writers. They are perpetually arrested in their pursuit of the various phantoms of art and individual expression. Being linked to the cultural traditions of Europe and the historical landscapes of Russia, they are also subject to bitter-amusing confrontations with the British or American cultural environment. In *The Real Life of Sebastian Knight* (1941), Nabokov's first novel in English, a writer called V. tries to establish purpose in life and art through his half-brother, the novelist Sebastian Knight who, after leaving Russia, settled in England. When he learns that Sebastian has died, he determines that there is a psychic message left for him, a revelation powerful enough to change his life. He feels that "the soul is but a manner of being - not a constant state." His identity becomes vague: "Sebastian's mask clings to my face, the likeness will not be washed off, I am Sebastian, or Sebastian is I, or perhaps we both are someone whom neither of us knows."[53] But Sebastian's "true" life eludes amid the paradoxes and puzzles of actuality and literature, just as it eluded Sebastian's biographer. V. acknowledges that people's "inner beings," let alone their verbal expressions, are inexplicable, deceitful and complex - that a "real" life does not exist.[54]

Humbert Humbert in *Lolita* (1955), a refined and sensitive middle-aged man of mixed European parentage, is similarly arrested in his own fantasies. In addition he is caught up in temporal fixations. His story, written in prison, tells of his long-standing passion for young girls, or nymphets, and the vexed relationship with one of them, the twelve-year-old Lolita. His obsession with this woman-child is the source of his ability to make the world obedient to his language-conscious imagination, to have an unrestrained perception of reality, a life-sustaining energy.

Though he operates on a different level of artistic imagination, Humbert Humbert resembles writer-characters of the period, an artist unable to protect himself against the snares and limitations of a life disconnected from moral norms, caught between innocence and experience, between pleasure and guilt. "Mr. Nabokov has given him a task that is almost too big for a fictional character," a reviewer writes in 1958 and suggests that "Humbert tends to run over into a figure of allegory, of Everyman."[55] Like Humbert Humbert, the writer-heroes of the 1950s and early 1960s typically represent literary Everyman arrested in the confusion of a new and powerful but strangely unformed and undirected imagination.

The idiosyncrasies of the writer-protagonist are more apparent in Nabokov's later work. In *Pale Fire* (1962) Charles Kinbote, an eccentric émigré teaching at an American college writes a commentary on the poem - called "Pale Fire" - by John Shade, the putative author, turning seemingly consistent events into a labyrinth of diverse interpretations. In an editorial foreword Kinbote insists that the poem has "no human reality" and that only his notes can provide it with necessary meaning.[56] Yet the exhaustive commentary and explanatory index he produces have precious little to do with the poem, which is not, as he claims, about King Charles and Zembla, an unidentified northern land. Kinbote misinterprets Shade and his work, confuses facts, and produces a parody of modern scholarship. He himself, in fact, is very likely a mad refugee named Botkin who imagines himself to be the exiled king of Zembla.

Just as Nabokov details a crazy-quilt of manipulated or shattered experience, several American novelists create similarly exuberant and emphatic visions. In John Barth's *The Floating Opera* (1956), published one year after *Lolita*, an oddly humorous and narcissistic character, Todd Andrews, sees life as being painfully arbitrary, insignificant, incomplete, a meaningless process in a blind universe.[*] He records his impressions in a mammoth personal chronicle called "Inquiry," a record

---

[*]The novel's original publishers insisted that Barth reduce its utter nihilism and provide a more encouraging (and ultimately unconvincing) ending. Barth returns to the original text in the Doubleday edition in 1967.

of disconnected meaningless fragments verging on entropy in which he sees a strangely satisfying and life-affirming process.

As we move into the fictions of the 1960s the determination of writers as heroes to abandon views on which they can rely and comprehend as verifiable fixities becomes more pronounced. Characters are increasingly ready to admit that life situations typically "exist" as illusion, that radical disorientation (frequently media enhanced) must be confronted and engaged. Undaunted, these writer-heroes are determined - despite long odds and in the midst of ontological uncertainty - to survive artistic crises. They reveal a willingness to employ various formal stratagems and patterns that reflect a quest for subjectivity and tentativeness.

Ebenezer Cooke, the hero of Barth's *The Sot-Weed Factor* (1960), is a case in point. A poet born in Maryland in the second half of the seventeenth century, raised and educated in England, then returned to America, he holds idealistic assumptions about the life and people of Maryland, where he plans to become a planter and "Poet and Laureate of the Province."[*] Yet his confident hopes are soon smashed when he is abused and cheated, indentured as a slave and captured by Indians. The duplicity and deception of those he meets confuse him utterly. The colony life reveals itself as a quagmire of violence, greed, prostitution and vulgarity: "Here's naught but scoundrels and perverts, hovels and brothels, corruption and poltroonery! What glory, to be singer of such a sewer!" Ebenezer comes to the realization that he held values that were naive and self-deceiving and concludes that life is a system of perpetual delusions and conspiracies. He decides to rewrite his poem, which he once intended to serve as a lofty accolade of colonial America, to

---

[*]The novel's hero, Ebenezer Cooke, is modelled after a poet by that name, the author of a poem called "The Sot-Weed Factor: Or, a Voyage to Maryland. A Satyr....in Burlesque Verse" (1708). Scant existing knowledge about the historical Cooke allows Barth to equip the fictional Cooke with an astoundingly adventurous and tortuous life in both colonial Maryland and England. The historical Cooke's later distortions of his poem, apparently to please the readers of the colony where he settled, gave Barth a convenient confirmation of what he intended to convey in his novel: history is a tangle of its own versions, a kind of fiction that absorbs changing myths and delusions.

express a scathing satire of the colony. In it he intends to "catalogue her every wickedness, and expose her every trap laid for the trusting, the unwary, the innocent!"[57] Conceding that the world is flawed but authentic and that the complexity of life is preferable to the "crime of innocence," he renounces thoughts of suicide and finds courage to regain his property.[58]

Bernie Gladhart, in James Purdy's *Cabot Wright Begins* (1964), who endeavors to investigate the life of a notorious rapist so as to write a bestselling novel, realizes that his hero is constantly eluding him. An impeccable gentleman with a hearing aid who collects clocks and lives in an unfurnished apartment, Cabot Wright does not fulfill anyone's expectations of a vicious criminal. He is, in fact, a puzzle to himself, layers of fictions and fantasies others have imposed on him. He has read so many versions of what he has done - raped more than three hundred women - that he can "safely affirm": "I couldn't remember what I did and what I didn't."[59] Though he distrusts writers and publishers, he agrees to assist them in order to expunge the falseness forced upon him: "If I could see my whole story written out straight, I think I could be cured."[60] This does in a sense take place. When the novel is completed, Cabot informs his biographers in a letter that he sees himself assembled in the book and therefore "free." As a result he can laugh, while before he could only giggle. But laughter has its precarious side-effects: it gives Cabot an erection, and that may mean more assaults on women. This curious psychological phenomenon, and his declaration that he will assume new roles (as a preacher in the South, or a medical quack) point to an uncertain "recovery." Gladhart and Zoe Bickle, the co-author, also face endless confusion and instability. Their writing is arrested, their theme is not fully explored. Distraught by bad reviews and by the fact that having lost Cabot she will never be able to write of him "as truth," Zoe declares: "I won't be a writer in a place and time like the present."[61]

Kurt Vonnegut's characters disclose a similarly transformed orientation and a loss of faith in the traditional American ethos. Howard W. Campbell, an American poet and playwright in *Mother Night* (1961), who served as a Nazi propaganda broadcaster in wartime Germany, but was also an American undercover agent, concedes that the two allegiances meant little to him. "All I can say is that I didn't believe them, that I knew full well what ignorant, destructive, obscenely jocular things I was saying."[62] What was important to him was his love for Helga, his German actress wife with whom he lived in an exclusive world they called "Das Reich der Zwei," "Nation of Two."[63] After Helga's death, Howard retreats to a "ratty attic" in New York City. When discovered and taken to Israel for trial, he writes his "confessions," the text of *Mother Night*. He admits that he has "lost the knack of making sense" and can only speak "gibberish to the civilized world."[64]

When John (or Jonah), the hero of Vonnegut's *Cat's Cradle* (1963), decides to write a book about what prominent Americans did on the day the atomic bomb destroyed Hiroshima he cannot predict his own entanglement in a "fictional" world characterized by vicious deception and appalling desolation. The entire population of San Lorenzo, the Caribbean island where the children of Felix Hoenikker (the inventor of the atomic bomb) now reside, lives in a world of pretensions, day-dreams, inventions and games. The rulers of the island conspire to keep the poverty-stricken people of San Lorenzo happy by creating a religion called Bokononism, and then making it illegal. In this way the natives are "all employed full time as actors in a play they understood....'So life became a work of art'...."[65] The ironic and paradoxical nature of the official religion is bluntly summed up in a statement that opens the "Book of Bokonon," a frivolously versified sacred writ claiming that nothing in it is true. John, who becomes a convert to Bokononism, admires the wisdom of the book and often refers to it. From a twice-divorced, chain-smoking alcoholic he turns into a faithful devotee of a theology that gives him a vision of "the unity of every second of all time and all wandering children."[66] As a writer he renounces his ambition to distinguish between reality and illusion. No longer a voice of knowledge, or verity, or a messenger of help, his new mission is to fulfil a "sacred obligation to produce beauty and enlightenment and comfort at top speed."[67] He feels that if life creates its own powerful fictions, a writer cannot help being an agent of them.

No longer burnt-out cases, like their counterparts in the 1950s, these early

1960s narrators are characteristically obsessional. Uncertain to what extent their vast, complex, confusing experiences can be used for personal awareness, or artistic benefit, suspicious of the efficacy of literature itself, these writers now find themselves manifesting extremism, irony, bitterness. Howard in *Mother Night* finds the world too malevolent to bear:

> The part of me that wanted to tell the truth got turned into an expert liar! The lover in me got turned into a pornographer! The artist in me got turned into ugliness such as the world has rarely seen before.[68]

The traditional novel, in which the writer has a position in society and certain stable philosophical convictions, in which he is in control of his art, and is ready to discuss all these, becomes a rare species. *Pictures from an Institution* (1954) by Randall Jarrell is a notable exception. It focuses on Gertrude Johnson, a novelist "between novels" who comes to Benton, a provincial but "progressive" college, to teach creative writing. An unpleasant person, conceited and contemptuous of anyone who is not a writer - "For her there were two species: writers and people; and the writers were really people, and the people weren't" - she upsets the Benton faculty but not Jarrold, a poet and teacher, and the novel's narrator.[69] Though he finds her amusing and has some sympathy for her mannerisms and eccentricity, he reprimands her, much as James castigated Flaubert, for writing without pity, for lacking compassion, for failing to understand, or to love, human weakness and folly. He disputes Gertrude's zeal for highly-crafted and elaborate writing built on orthodox syntax and grammar, and he scorns her heavily-wrought plot, which she finds necessary to give plausibility to the implausible characters of ordinary experience. Jarrold's own roman á clef of Benton functions as a foil to Gertrude's effort. Renouncing formal structure or a sustained plot, his anti-narrative occurs as a series of flashbacks that disclose the fragmentation and dislocation of experience. It foregrounds the elusive and unconscious elements of the quotidian struggle, yet dispels the conviction that evil pervades everything but the mind of the writer.

But *Pictures from an Institution* does not confront the conflict of these opposing sensibilities as part of a larger crisis of postwar moral and artistic perception. Jarrell's characters are, like Gertrude's vision of Benton, isolated geographically and psychologically from the undercurrents of creative blockage that haunted the postwar decade.

A more complex view of an intellectual faced with artistic paralysis and pessimism appears in Saul Bellow's *Herzog* (1964). Moses Herzog, a man of letters (quite literally) corresponds with friends and various personages, living and dead, to overcome the mental crisis caused by a mixture of private failures and the perceived decline of Western culture by "scrawling" letters and yielding to the "excitement that inspired it."[70] He sees a need to step beyond old possibilities, refuses to be a victim of immobility and frustration at the time when people see themselves merely as "survivors." The intellectual poseur, who is "safe, comfortable...playing at crisis, alienation, apocalypse and desperation" fills him with disdain. He believes he should "have the power to employ pain, to repent, to be illuminated."[71] As the novel closes, Herzog declares that his depression, "whatever had come over him during these last months, the spell, really seemed to be passing, really going."[72]

Willis Mosby, in "Mosby's Memoirs" (1968), another notable Bellow hero of the 1960s, also signals a desire to transform modern defeatism into strength. An aging diplomat, a man of pride and studied detachment, Mosby is uncomfortable both with the world as it is and the limitations of his writing. He would like to walk out of the image he has constructed, a "separate creation" entombed in writing, "a finished product...in this cogitating, unlaughing, stone, iron, nonsensical form." He engages in a fantasy in which he had died some years earlier and now his "doom was to live life to the end as Mosby," a kind of purgatory of unreality in which men "grow ugly" under "imperative tasks" and "monstrous compulsions of duty."[73]

Mosby and Herzog record the psychic and intellectual chaos of their time and claim, uncertainly but doggedly, that they will not succumb. Yet their confusion is not yet reworked into viable modes of creativity. Like most heroes of the 1950s and the early 1960s, they cannot imagine effective strategies of escape. Their perception remains directed inward rather than outward or forward. While these tormented heroes deplore the disintegration of traditional values and authentic social roles, an emerging class of literary characters begins to exploit such confusion by re-imagining the past and re-making the present, or by de-mythicizing culture and deflating art's pretensions. They are prepared to rework loss and void into new and bold visions of life and radical experiments in language.

NOTES

1.Michiko Kakutani, "The Hero as Writer," *New York Times Book Review*, July 11, 1982.

2.Patricia Hampl, *A Romantic Education* (Boston: Houghton Mifflin, 1981), p.10.

3.John Irving, *The World According to Garp* (New York: Dutton, 1978). p.63.

4.Saul Bellow, *Humboldt's Gift* (New York: The Viking Press, 1975), p.163.

5.Maurice Beebe, *Ivory Towers and Sacred Founts: The Artist as Hero in Fiction from Goethe to Joyce* (Purdue University, New York University Press, 1964), pp.vi, 307-8.

6.Ibid., pp.308, vi.

7. Lee T. Lemon, *Portraits of the Artist in Contemporary Fiction* (Lincoln and London: University of Nebraska Press, 1985), pp. ix-xiii.

8.Philip Roth, *Operation Shylock* (1993; London: Vintage, 1994), p.86.

9.John W. Aldridge, *In Search of Heresy: American Literature in an Age of Conformity* (New York: McGraw-Hill, 1956), p.12.

10.Irving Howe, "The age of conformity," *Partisan Review*, papers of a symposium printed in several issues of the magazine in 1952.

11.Van Wyck Brooks, *The Writer in America* (New York: Avon Books, 1964), pp. 175, 181, 186.

12.John W. Aldridge, *After the Lost Generation: a Critical Study of the Writers of Two Wars* (New York: McGraw-Hill, 1951), p.238.

13.Cowley, Malcolm, "New Times, New Values," *New Republic*, August 16, 1954.

14.Irving Howe, *Decline of the New* (New York: Horizon Press, 1978), pp.196-200.

15.Wystan Hugh Auden, "Henry James and the Artist in America," *Harper's*, July, 1948.

16.Henry Miller, *Tropic of Cancer* (New York: Grove, 1961), p.245.

17.Henry Miller, "The Alcoholic Veteran with the Washboard Cranium" in *Nights of Love and Laughter* (New York: Signet, The New American Library, 1955), p.26-27.

18.Ibid., p.40.

19.Saul Bellow, *Mosby's Memoirs and Other Stories* (New York: The Viking Press, 1968), pp. 132, 113.

20.Ibid., pp.122-23.

21.Ibid., p. 123-124.

22.Ibid., pp.133-142.

23.Norman Mailer *Barbary Shore* (1951; New York: Howard Fertig, 1980), pp.9-10.

24.Ibid., p. 311.

25.Norman Mailer, *The Deer Park* (New York: Putnam, 1955), p.47.

26.Ibid., p.353.

27.Ibid., p.100.

28.Ibid., p.326.

29.Norman Mailer, *Advertisements for Myself* (New York: Putnam, 1959), p.158.

30.Ibid., pp.169, 179, 159.

31.Ibid., p.184.

32.Ibid., p.179.

33.Ibid., p.184.

34.Ernest Hemingway, *The Garden of Eden* (New York: Scribner's, 1986), p.193.

35.Ibid., p. 193.

36.Sylvia Plath, *The Bell Jar* (London: Faber and Faber, 1963), pp.126, 196.

37.Jack Kerouac, *On the Road* (1957; New York: Signet, 1985), pp.47, 8, 53.

38.Ibid., p.66.

39.Jack Kerouac, *Dharma Bums* (1958; Harmondsworth: Penguin, 1976), p.97.

40.Ibid., p.200.

41.Jack Kerouac, *The Subterraneans* (New York: Grove Press, 1958), p.70.

42.Ibid., p.1.

43.John Clellon Holmes, *Go* (New York: Thunder's Mouth Press, 1988), p.98.

44.Ibid., p.68.

45.Ibid., pp.32, 68.

46.Ibid., p.70.

47.Tom Wolfe, *The Electric Kool-Aid Acid Test* (1968; New York: Bantam, 1969), pp.8, 41, 93.

48.Ibid., pp. 91, 127.

49.Ibid., p.183.

50.Ibid., p.370.

51.Tony Tanner, *City of Words* (New York: Harper and Row, 1971), p.115.

52.William Burroughs, *Queer* (New York: Viking, 1985), p.xvi.

53.Vladimir Nabokov, *The Real Life of Sebastian Knight* (Norfolk, Conn.: New Directions, 1959), p.204-5.

54. Ibid., p.66.

55.Elizabeth Janeway, in the review of *Lolita* in *The New York Times*, August 17, 1958.

56.Vladimir Nabokov, *Pale Fire* (1962; New York: Berkley Books, 1968), p.12.

57.John Barth, *The Sot-Weed Factor* (1960; New York: Grosset, 1964), pp.483-84.

58.Ibid., p.788.

59.James Purdy, *Cabot Wright Begins* (New York: Farrar, Straus and Giroux, 1964), p.93.

60.Ibid., p.96.

61.Ibid., p.228.

62.Kurt Vonnegut, *Mother Night* (1961; New York: Dell, 1974), p.133.

63.Ibid., p.37.

64.Ibid., p.96.

65.Kurt Vonnegut, *Cat's Cradle* (New York: Holt, Rinehart and Winston, 1963), p.144.

66.Ibid., p.67.

67.Ibid., p.189.

68.Kurt Vonnegut, *Mother Night*, p.150.

69.Randall Jarrell, *Pictures from an Institution* (New York: Knopf, 1954), p.22.

70.Saul Bellow, *Herzog* (1964; Greenwich, Conn.: Fawcett Crest Book, 1965), p.9-10.

71.Ibid., pp.385-86.

72.Ibid., p.415.

73.Saul Bellow, "Mosby's Memoirs" in *Mosby's Memoirs and Other Stories*, pp.182-84.

CHAPTER ONE

WE IMPROVISE OUR NOVELS
AS WE IMPROVISE OUR LIVES

NO SANCTION OF A CREATOR

The 1960s is the time of superpower confrontations and political assassinations, of waging an unpopular war, of campus conflicts and racial tensions. American writers react to these developments. They denounce the government and the military, criticize the country's moral and cultural decadence, blame the media (especially television), for deceiving and numbing their audience. Tradition, history and culture in general are described as fictive, fraudulently shaped by debased language and self-serving, often discredited, ideology. Consequently, radical experimentation occurs within the medium of fiction itself. The novel's conventional meaning and form are renounced as irrelevant, exhausted or dead. Writers attempt to renew the novel partly by parody and pastiche, by employing radical irony, self-consciousness and reflexivity, by blending high art with popular culture. Their major subject is now often the act of creation itself as well as the application of it to the redefining of traditional perception, history or morality. Realistic representation and objectivity are replaced by appeals to fantasy, arbitrariness, disruption. Fiction about writers and writing functions as a frontier of artistic inquiry, the test of literary verity whose legitimacy often depends, Jerome Klinkowitz observes, "solely upon how persuasively that account is stated."[1]

To make order in the convulsive dissensions and transformations of the novelistic hero of the 1960s remains problematic, nor can one easily ascertain precisely where the various "sixties" phenomena actually begin or end. Some of them are evident in the 1950s, others become distinct only towards the end of the 1960s. Many are continued or developed in the seventies or the eighties. Yet the year 1968 is usually seen as the postmodernist watershed which produced Sukenick's *Up*, Richard Brautigan's *In Watermelon Sugar*, Steve Katz's *The Exaggerations of Peter Prince*, William H. Gass' *In the Heart of the Heart of the Country*, John Barth's *Lost in the Funhouse*, Mailer's *The Armies of the Night*, to mention only a few. In these texts, and in others like them, meta or surfiction is no longer limited to parodying contemporary life and history to "a kind of absurd comic strip" but now becomes the site of imaginative and innovative reworkings.[2]

Characteristically, the above-mentioned fictions also inaugurate non-traditional writer-heroes, characters that reveal themselves as imaginative and enthusiastic inventors of literary visions and as destroyers of a falsely reliable and used-up intellectual tradition. Though they complain, like their predecessors, of a sense of emptiness, of the grotesqueness and absurdity of life in America, they are much less withdrawn, less aimless in their attempts to transform failures into advantages. They are more imaginative and focus on the unconventionality of their attitudes, on the importance of eccentric and disruptive lifestyles, on the attractions of human sexuality.

Manifesting radically self-conscious authorial personae in the late 1960s, the postmodernist novel often depends on the extent to which language itself is demystified. Writers such as Donald Barthelme, William Gass, Robert Coover, Thomas Pynchon and Walter Abish do not record or mirror life but create, or negotiate, visions of reality in which articulation is random and insignificant. They use verbal structures that lead to more verbal structures, in which elusive narrators, frequently reduced to voices, modes of consciousness, or methods of composition, parody, negate, or annihilate themselves rather than prevail as authorial presences.

In Barthelme's fiction, for example, the authorial persona is replaced by a disassembling voice, or an energy, a non-bodily articulation fervently orchestrating collaged visions too tangled to be rendered through conventional language. He (it) prefers to be what the narrative voice in *Snow White* (1967), remembers his father had told him to be, "a man about whom nothing is known"[3] (an obvious parody of James' advice: the writer is a person "on whom nothing is lost") or, what a character of another story wants to be, a "double-minded man."[4] In Walter Abish's *Alphabetical Africa* (1974), chapters contain only words beginning with letters which have been alphabetically designated (for example, in chapter "B" the words all start with "a" or "b"); consequently, characters have to wait until their letter comes up. Consequently, the first-person narrator can only speak in chapter "I." In a similarly arranged *Splendide-Hôtel* (1973), by Gilbert Sorrentino, the narrating voice of chapter "I" thus belittles the concept of a literary persona:

> One imagines this comfortable son of a bitch thinking of himself as Arthur Rimbaud. As he places that *I* on the paper he is, in all his mediocrity, more puissant than the shade that he has turned into a "character."[5]

Earlier, the letter "b" - "The sound an idiot makes" - provokes the narrating voice to deny language the power to convey truth and emotion and declare that the writer, a "contemptible" concept, is faced with verbal ineptitude and impotence:

> The language...is dead, a smell of putrefaction hangs over it. The poet, idiot of artifact, punches his face, babbles, b-b-b-b....The wonder is that any artist stays sane.[6]

James Kunen similarly derides his own *The Strawberry Statement* (1969) in a slapstick and self-mocking manner:

> The best, truest way to read this book would be to rip it up and throw the scraps all over the house. Then later, should you come across a piece, read it, or don't read it, depending upon how you feel. Or, better, save it until four a o'clock in the morning when you would rather do almost anything else, and read it then. Above all, don't spend too much time reading it because I didn't

spend too much time writing it.[7]

Teasing the reader, thwarting his expectations, is not enough for Kunen. He deprecates his own presence in the book, shows himself as a ridiculously flawed author:

> This book was written on napkins and cigarette packs and hitchhiking signs. It was spread all over, but so is my mind. I exhibit a marked tendency to forget things. I can remember only three things at a time."[8]

Deprived of convincing characterization, truncated as literary protagonists, such shadows of authors as characters, or rather verbal expressions imitating characters, act as conscious subverters of the principles and creeds of the literary tradition. They are not coherent personalities, rather fragments of selves, often contradictory, frequently nameless. The narrator of Richard Brautigan's *In Watermelon Sugar* (1968) insists that "My name depends on you" and claims his life is "done in watermelon sugar." When asked by members of the community of iDEATH to describe the book he is writing, he is able to say only "Just what I'm writing down: one word after another." He adds that it is not going to be like the "terrible books" people used to write in the land of "the Forgotten Works."[9]

When among the many digressions in *Snow White* the question "Where is the figure in the carpet?" is asked, the answer is only a hint that what we deal with is "just...carpet," also that asking such questions is "a lot of buffalo hump."[10] To many postmodernist writers, "experience is 'just carpet,'" observes David Lodge, "and whatever patterns we discern in it are wholly illusory, comforting fictions."[11]

Such fascination with fragmented, incomplete and oblique representation, with paradox, pastiche and collage becomes in these and other similarly "rigorous" metafictional works a creative cul-de-sac that utterly thwarts the enquiry into the condition of being a writer. The authorly articulations are circumscribed by captivities and convolutions of an obsessive addiction to the purity of means.

Personality is not embraced, lives are devoid of inner existence, flattened, confined to elusive identities, turned into types, linguistic entities, symbols. They remain as fragmented and jumbled as the prose that sustains them. Social and cultural backgrounds are impoverished, or meaningless. Narrating voices do not enjoy the freedom they first envisioned, nor do they acquire unusual imaginative power.*

Other leading representatives of American postmodernism, including Raymond Federman, Ronald Sukenick, John Barth**, Kurt Vonnegut, or the later Philip Roth, are less stubbornly attached to the purity of metafictional narrative. Without abandoning radical self-reflexivity and formal experimentation, they employ characters that resemble conventional literary figures, or actual persons (frequently the authors themselves), who live in, and often refer to, the contemporary American scene, who use freely what Sorrentino dismissingly called literature's obscuring "signals": "conversation, physiognomy, clothing, accoutrements, possessions, social graces."[12] Blending a reliance on illusion and a search for new techniques of realism, vacillating between constructs of metafiction and

---

*Dissatisfaction with fiction that favors experimentation at the cost of meaning, plot or character description occasionally occurs in the pages of novels that are themselves given to experimental techniques. A metafictional writer named Helmbart (whom Jerome Klinkowitz recognizes as "an obvious play on the occasional duo-syllabic pronunciation of Donald Barthelme's last name"), the author of a novel called *Vital Telegrams*, described as "almost a story of sentence structure rather than of characters," is declared by the narrator of John Irving's *The Water-Method Man* as being unreadable and worthless. Similarly, the writer-character in Kosinski's *The Hermit of 69th Street* while pondering the possibility of writing a novel about "the making of the Nouveau Roman" is told by the Kosinski persona: "You could....But who would want to read it?" [Jerome Klinkowitz, *Literary Subversions: New American Fiction and the Practice of Criticism* (Carbondale: Southern Illinois Univ. Press, 1985), p.35; John Irving, *The Water-Method Man* (New York: Random House, 1972), pp.243-44; Jerzy Kosinski, *The Hermit of 69th Street* (New York: Zebra, 1991), p.51.]

**Jerome Klinkowitz thinks Barth is given more to the Aristotelian aesthetic than to the genuine spirit of change and quest. The way he describes the novelist supports the view that to look for viable images of writer-heroes in recent fiction we have to turn first to those authors who do not strive to "suspend the suspension of disbelief." Barth is not among them. He, according to Klinkowitz, "much prefers fictions which represent something existing in the world - fictions in which the things that happen are metaphors for something else, not something in themselves. For Barth, it seems, fiction should forever be an imitation of an action, and not an action in itself." [Jerome Klinkowitz, *Literary Subversions: New American Fiction and the Practice of Criticism* (Carbondale: Southern Illinois University Press, 1985), p.14.]

autobiographical factuality, these characters provide the writer-hero fiction after 1968 with new and exuberant formal-thematic possibilities.

The writer in Ronald Sukenick's *Up* (1968), for example, avoids chronological development, reliability, even consistent grammatical identity - at one point he simulates briefly a different identity - yet he calls himself "Sukenick" and insists on his bond with the author of *Up*. The existence and validity of his book, he argues, depend on his ability to contain within its bounds the flux and disparity of experience, to go on and finish his work, to resist the skeptical voices he has created for himself under the guise of the novel's other characters. "Seriously, it doesn't go anywhere....this is just a collection of disjointed fragments. You don't get anywhere at all....It's all words and nothing but words," he muses, and then asks himself: "Are we children reading fairy tales or men trying to work out the essentials of our fate?"[13] An elemental antagonism is at work in such trickery, a rejection of artistic certainty and a hope to build it anew, a dichotomy which Raymond Federman calls "the construction of a fictional illusion and the laying bare of that illusion."[14]

As the action, along with its modes of narration, perspectives, tone and mood change, so does the author-hero of *Up*. He is a personality that is elusive, mercurial, mutable, but also an artist aware that he can perform on unexplored levels of creative possibility. What "art is all about," the Sukenick persona declares, is "the invention of reality," not its discovery - the important difference being that multiplicity informs "inventing," while discovering implies finality. He explains that

> Art seeks a vital connection with the world that, to stay alive, must be constantly reinvented to correspond with our truest feelings....Art is a process of self-creation. It literally brings you to life.[15]

When a friend calls a girl they both know "a raving maniac" who "makes up her own version of everything as she goes along," Sukenick-the-character replies: "Don't we all?"[16] He is obsessively eager to invent his own mutations, psychic and artistic, visions that could take place in the life of a young writer who wants to approach experience in a fresh and authentic manner.

Up lacks formal and thematic closure. The Sukenick persona ends as he began, uncertainly, searchingly, shyly, with comic exuberance and self-denial that are, nevertheless, designated by an outer sense of verity and actuality. At a party to celebrate the end of his novel, he declares that he is "just playing with words anyway....Just playing with words ga-ga-ga-ga-ga-ga-goo-goo-gig-geg-gug-gack," then he vows he is after veracity and cohesion: "Though it's all true what I've written, every word of it, I insist on that."[17]

Postmodernist writer-heroes stress their own being as a construction in the making. They frequently repudiate earlier practices and experiences so as to assume new ones. Occasionally, they disrupt their tales to confront the reader, or to check what he makes of the story line, or to append new ideas. In William Gass' *Willie Master's Lonesome Wife* (1971) the reader is unexpectedly ridiculed: "You've been had, haven't you, jocko? you sad stew-faced sonofabitch. Really, did you read this far? puzzle your head? turn the pages this and that, around about? Was it racy enough to suit? There wasn't much plot?"[18] In *Snow White*, Barthelme interrupts the story to ask a list of questions concerning the contents of the text. Some of the numbered questions are extreme in scope, others irrelevant and confusing. He wants to know, for example: "8. Would you like a war? Yes( ) No( ), 13. Holding in mind all works of fiction since the War, in all languages, how would you rate the present work, on a scale of one to ten, so far?"[19] In the middle of Federman's *Take It or Leave It* (1976), the narrating voice ends a similar list of questions by asking whether the reader has already seen such a questionnaire, and "If so where?" On the previous page Federman includes the note: "[courtesy SNOW WHITE]."[20] In *The Hermit of 69th Street* (1988), the reader is asked to reflect, for at least six minutes, on such weighty questions as why there is life, and whether man's fall is inevitable. Kosinski and his hero, Kosky, regularly interrupt their loosely-linked ideas and biographical episodes with literally thousands of annotations and quotations, thus obliging the reader to consider the implications, associations, or ramifications of the extrinsic material *vis á vis* the "narrative."

Such transformations and ploys are needed, writer-heroes insist, to meet the changing circumstances of life and shifting demands of art. The writer cannot be the custodian of approved moral stances and dated literary conventions. In his *The Death of the Novel and Other Stories* (1969) Sukenick reasons:

> No, we have to invent new games - and then discard them and invent more. This, then, is the beginning of our literary re-education. A story is a game someone has played so that you can play it too, and having learned how to play it, throw it away. All good books are both didactic and gratuitous. I want to write a book that will teach things I don't know.[21]

In *Out* (1973), Sukenick similarly suggests that the writer's attempt to assemble life's fleeting moments into some creative recognition is an ongoing endeavor: "I want to write a book like a cloud that changes as it goes." This does not, however, lead to stability and order but to formlessness and, inevitably, devastation. The characters of *Out* are a group of revolutionaries (or terrorists) travelling across the country, running away from some unspecified oppression, carrying out mysterious missions, using explosives to destroy the existing order. One of the men, Empty Fox, declares:

> I want to erase all books. My ambition is to unlearn everything I can't read or write....I want to unlearn and unlearn till I get to the place where the ocean of the unknown begins where my fathers live.[22]

As the events of the novel become increasingly outlandish and meaningless, the Sukenick persona states that he is not in control of what happens on the pages of his own book. At the end, as the characters, even the text, eliminate themselves, become blank unprinted spaces, he has his name transmuted to Roland Sycamore, then reduced to the initial "R" only.

In Raymond Federman's fiction, characters, which are both imaginative constructs and personae resembling their real-world author, are similarly self-annulling in their pursuit of new mental-artistic possibilities. Federman thus alludes to, and distinguishes himself from, the imaginary world of Sukenick:

I want to write a book like a cloud that changes as it goes he said.

I want to tell a story that cancels itself as it goes I replied.[23]

The attempt to go beyond the existing possibilities of metafiction, including one's own, is increasingly manifest in Federman's novels. In *Double or Nothing* (1971) several voices are involved in the telling of the story of a nineteen-year-old émigré who comes to the States from France after the Second World War. Among them is a "somewhat paranoic fellow," a solitary scribe who intends to lock himself in a room for a year to write.[24] He is so pre-occupied with this self-imposed literary task, and so confused by the conflicting visions of his protagonist that the actual telling of his story becomes for him a hopeless, infinitely elusive undertaking, while he himself is reduced to an absurd figure trapped in a fictitious labyrinth.

Federman's *The Twofold Vibration* (1982), similarly contains characters, or composite narrative presences, that oddly expand and contradict themselves. "Federman" (not "federman," a sign that in his later work Federman moves towards a more cohesive, biographical view of himself) is the writer-narrator who, with the help of two assistants, Namredef and Moinous, is involved in putting together a story of an old friend, also a writer, a survivor of the Holocaust and a bilingual French immigrant, who is being deported to space colonies.* All three characters want the

---

*Federman explains at the beginning of *The Twofold Vibration* that the book is not "futuristic crap...pseudoscientific bullshit, space warfare...no gadgetry, no crass emotionless robots...none of this infantilism." It is, rather, he suggests, a kind of an ambitious experiment, "exploratory or better extemporaneous fiction." His dismissal of science-fiction devices reflects a larger prejudice. Outer space, space technology, or science-fiction in general are rarely employed by authors of writer-novels, save those novels that are classified as science-fiction per se. Burroughs is obviously an exception, but his outer space invaders cannot be seen as coherent referents to his elusive writer image. American novelists prefer to focus on manipulating their heroes in time rather than in space, in the present rather than in the future, in social relations rather than in technological or fantastic environments. [*The Twofold Vibration*, (Bloomington: Indiana Univ. Press, 1982), pp.1-2.]

story to be true and complete but, as in the previous novels, its themes prove elusive. Federman, the novel's author, and the various "Federmans" of his texts, propose that writing, seemingly a form of truth, cannot express the flux of experience. Rather, instead of being experience itself, it is a contrived process reflecting the paradoxes of literary creation, a rehearsal of the imaginative but unfixed possibilities of the writer and the reader, as well as a display of the limitations of language.

Similarly, Paul Auster's writer-heroes ultimately investigate, and invalidate, themselves and their writing. In *The New York Trilogy* (1985) they become detectives who obsessively engage in obscure missions and grotesque rituals which bring them to the point of psychic/artistic self-destruction. In *City of Glass*, the first part of the trilogy, Quinn, once an ambitious writer and critic, is mistaken by a late night caller for a detective named Paul Auster. Not to disillusion the caller, Quinn takes the case offered to him. Soon, he finds himself in pursuit of Stillman, a man who has been striving to invent a new paradise by redefining ways in which language and meaning reflect reality. When the elusive Stillman disappears, Quinn takes up residence in the now empty apartment of the people who hired him. He eats food that mysteriously appears there, sleeps and writes in his red notebook. In it, he tries to express himself as economically and clearly as possible and regrets "having wasted so many pages at the beginning." In fact, he is "sorry that he had bothered to write about the Stillman case at all." He feels that "his words had been severed from him, that now they were a part of the world at large." When Paul Auster - who turns out to be a writer rather than a detective - and a friend try to find out about the mysterious Quinn and his red notebook they are confused, discouraged, unable to "even hazard a guess."[25]

In *The Locked Room*, from the above trilogy, the protagonist is asked to examine the literary work of Fanshawe, a childhood friend of his who has left his wife and son and has not been seen for years (references to Hawthorne and other "ghosts" of literature are frequent in Auster's prose). He not only publishes the riches Fanshawe left, but also marries his wife and adopts his son. Soon, however, he feels he is haunted by his missing friend. To reestablish control over himself, he decides to write Fanshawe's biography and kill him in it, as well as to actually find and confront the man. After the two writers meet and engage in a bizarre fight in Paris (the protagonist claims he is Herman Melville while Fanshawe insists his name is Peter Stillman), the elusive Fanshawe resolves to see the narrator for the last time. He produces a red notebook which, though recognized by the protagonist, seems to be filled with words that are "put together strangely, as though their final purpose was to cancel each other out."[26] As in *The City of Glass*, the categories of author, narrator and reader are subverted and blurred while a peculiar, perplexing correlation between literature's "selves" and the reader's inability to escape their control is somberly foregrounded.

Typically, the writer hero in these and other metafictional novels aspires to more than escape from social and cultural actuality, or to re-formulate the rules of conduct and perception, as the Beat writers did a decade earlier. He strives to achieve some new, constantly reworked, instinctively achieved, mental-literary optics for his times, and he wants to capture them in forms that are not conditioned by the traditional patterns of the novel. To accomplish these he assumes the unique responsibility proposed in *A Portrait of the Artist as a Young Man*: to replace God as the master-shaper of human perception of reality. Sukenick explains:

> The contemporary writer - the writer who is acutely in touch with the life of which he is a part - is forced to start from scratch: Reality doesn't exist, personality doesn't exist, time doesn't exist. God was the omniscient author, but he died; now no one knows the plot, and since our reality lacks the sanction of a creator, there's no guarantee as to the authenticity of the received version....[27]

To live up to such a role the metafictional writer-hero insists on functioning as not only a re-interpreter or re-organizer of reality but also its manipulator, or inventor. He calls himself a literary magician, or juggler, or trickster. According to Sukenick writers are "master jugglers...artists in the sense that circus performers are called artists, equilibrists who can do seven things at once without thinking about it."[28] Barth is a "Genie" who returns to the time of the fabled Scheherazade, then fades in and out of her life. Vonnegut as a fictional character wears mirrored glasses in order to pass "incognito" among his own characters. Auster's hero feels he is "the sublime alchemist who could change the world at will."[29] Roth's Zuckerman claims he is a troupe of players, "a permanent company of actors that I can call upon when a self is required."[30]

In Joan Didion's *Democracy* (1984), the writer is the classifier and interpreter of what fills people's thoughts: elements of visual imagery derived from films, advertizing, print, and tv. The Didion persona tries to arrange the broken fragments by which her characters briefly reveal themselves. She reconstructs their puzzling thoughts and actions so as to put them into "that suspended judgement in which a novel is written." She is an investigator, an assembler of the human jig-saw puzzle. Her material is not life but "players," "versions," "performances," "tricks."

> In the summer of 1975 each of the major and minor players still had a stake in his or her own version of recent events, and I spent the summer collecting and collating these versions, many of them conflicting, most of them self-serving; an essentially reportorial technique.[31]

Didion-the-character compares herself to a tightrope walker, an "aerialist" who reminds herself to avoid looking down. The image is fitting. Concentrating on her feat (or feet) she is aware of the tenuousness of both her performance and her existence as artistic possibility. "You see the shards of the novel I am no longer writing, the island, the family, the situation. I lost patience with it. I lost nerve" confesses Didion early in *Democracy* and echoes of her frustration reverberate throughout the novel.[32] She says finally: "It has not been the novel I set out to write, nor am I exactly the person who set out to write it."[33]

The postmodernist writer-heroes' compulsion to perform as a literary master-magician is shadowed by an apprehension that authorial superiority is limited, artistically and ontologically, and reduced to largely uncontrollable and unpredictable imaginative ploys. They are aware that writing does not yield a lasting relevance, that they cannot privilege a given interpretation or maintain an illusion. "Story-teller Strangled By Own Yarn. Why do all our inventions become Frankensteins," wonders the writer persona in *The Death of the Novel and Other Stories*. At the end of the book he hears himself say: "Everything's blowing up, falling to pieces. Art dissolves back into life. Chaos. It's not the way I planned it."[34]

John Barth asserts that to explore the structures and devices of fiction one is faced with an ongoing conflict between creative excitement and intense anxiety, between play and dread.* In the title story of *Lost in the Funhouse* (1968), Ambrose Mensch, a thirteen-year-old boy with the imagination of a future writer, explains how the Ocean City funhouse becomes a literary metaphor that is both fascinating and alienating. Ambrose is confused by the structure of the funhouse, frustrated by his inability to reach its promised fun sections. He wishes he had never encountered its perceptions and effects, and he finally resolves to become the constructor of "funhouses for others and be their secret operator - though he would rather be among the lovers** for whom funhouses are designed."[35]

Lost in the Funhouse further reveals how the new writer transcends the rigidities of life only to be faced with regret, self-pity, doubt. In "Life-Story" an author of stories and novels finds being a character in his own narrative a mode of entrapment:

---

*The conflict between the need to invent or control reality as a fictional construct and the fear that one has been upstaged by other forces is also expressed in works in which authorial presences are consciously reduced or even eliminated. "I wander the island, inventing it," claims a nameless authorial voice at the beginning of Robert Coover's "The Magic Poker." A moment later it adds: "But anything can happen." As the story progresses, the voice engages in similarly disparate assumptions. It assumes divine authority: "perhaps tomorrow I will invent Chicago and Jesus Christ...Just as I have invented you," or recoils into uncertainty and diffidence: "This is awkward...I don't know....To tell the truth, I sometimes wonder if it was not he [one of the characters] who invented me...." [Robert Coover, *Pricksongs and Descants* (New York: New American Library, 1969), pp.20-40.]

**"It is clear in the *Funhouse*," observes Robert Scholes, "that being an artist is [for Barth] only a poor substitute for being a lover." However, typically for postmodernist narrators the Barthian hero sees much of the frustration of being an artist compensated by erotic play and metaphor. [Robert Scholes, "The Allegory of Exhaustion," *Fiction International*, #1, Fall, 1973, p.107.]

Another story about a writer writing a story! Another regressus in infinitum! Who doesn't prefer art that at least overtly imitates something other than its own processes?[36]

He regrets he was not born in the age of realistic fiction characterized by "passion and bravura action."[37] The experimental fictions of Beckett or Borges, the theater of the absurd, black humor do not appeal to him. But questions raised by these authors are troubling. Is the world itself not a novel, a fiction in which he is a character? Is it possible to verify what is real and what is fiction, or what a writer fictionalizes and what is fictionalized for him? Like Ambrose from "Lost in the Funhouse" he is aware of the discords in the funhouse of fiction, except he is a seasoned practitioner of illusion who fears that self-consciousness ultimately leads to self-negation and absurdity.

While expressing such grievances and fears the various writer-characters, or voices, in *Lost in the Funhouse* betray the desire to discover ways of renovating the existing workings of the literary imagination. Barth's next work, *Chimera* (1972), delineates a solution. The Genie, a Barth-like writer-spirit, explains that the "exhaustion" of the novel* can be salvaged by restoring the genre, "by some magic," to "the original springs of narrative." "The key to the treasure" is "the treasure," he discovers (as time traveller) in his rendezvous with Scheherazade; the remaking of existing stories, multiplying them, juggling them is the reality of the story.[38] Writing, like the Chimera, is a "creature of the imagination, any impossible or monstrous fancy."**

Nabokov's characters, at a loss amid alien language and culture, survive by radically interpreting experience. As liars, maniacs, or madmen they relate stories that radically obscure coherent or determinate meaning. Describing *Pale Fire* (1962)

---

* Barth's term in his prominently publicized 1967 essay "The Literature of Exhaustion"

**John Barth's own definition of the term in an introduction to a reading from *Chimera*. [John Barth, *The Friday Book* (New York: Putnam's Sons, 1984), p.97.]

as a "Jack-in-the-box, a Fabergé gem, a clockwork toy, a chess problem, an infernal machine, a trap to catch reviewers, a cat-and-mouse game, a do-it-yourself novel," Mary McCarthy points to the murky side of bewilderment and inventiveness in the Nabokovian funhouse: "Each plane or level in its shadow box proves to be a false bottom; there is an infinite perspective regression, for the book is a book of mirrors...but the real, real story, the story underneath, has been transpiring gradually, by degrees to the reader. Kinbote is mad."[39]

In *Look at the Harlequins!* (1974) reliability is radically undercut by madness. Vadim Vadimovich N., an Anglo-Russian writer who tries to retain order and sanity through an "endless recreation" of his "fluid self," believes that dementia is "one of the characters in my story."[40] His biography, entitled *Look at the Harlequins!*, is a succession of complaints concerning psychic aberrations and self-torments. He is confused about directions like left and right and harbors a persistent suspicion that he is merely a shadow, a variant, and thus a parody, of another, more talented writer of Russian origin. When he finally suffers a mysterious paralysis, a death-like coma, he discovers his original identity, his real name, a sense of sanity. Yet VV is a schizoid character, a madman. The reality which, he thinks, he has regained is a fictional existence, a world of obsessive fantasy again, another pain-or-death-oriented mirror image of himself.

Yet few novelists share Nabokov's penchant for enquiry into realms of utter unreliability. Their author-heroes are tame by comparison; they are less obscure and self-mocking - less haunted by the past. Moving into the 1980s, American novelists are more factual and pragmatic, more involved in the contemporary social-political American scene.

In Barth's *Sabbatical* (1982) protagonists Fenn and Susan Turner, a married couple involved in writing a novel which may turn out to be *Sabbatical* itself, share the view that life in America is controlled by institutionalized conspiracies, that ordinary existence has become untrustworthy and confusing. Refusing to be overwhelmed by the country's outer chaos, trusting there must be some convincing patterns linking art and life, eager, like other Barth characters, to revise life and to make it better, they decide to embark on a nine-month sea cruise to the Caribbean and back. Their sabbatical - she is on a leave from her university, he, suspended between careers, aspires to establish himself as a writer - is both a flight and the unfolding narrative.

Aware that they have to rely on themselves during their uncertain, often dangerous floating, both literal and metaphorical, the Turners stress the importance of the search for meaning through the creative process. Barth's obsession with situations which perpetuate themselves through words (as in the Moebius strip[*] structure in *Lost in the Funhouse*) obtains in *Sabbatical*:

> If that's going to be our story, then lets begin it at the end and end at the beginning, so we can go on forever.[41]

Inevitably, the Turners fail to reconcile life with art. What they learn is that the indeterminacy of life cannot be circumvented by literary patterning, that human existence is, in spite of its peculiar parables, analogies and symbols, a discontinuous and elusive affair - informed by too many turns. *Sabbatical* offers a pattern that Barth himself, and a number of other novelists, have employed since the sixties. A writer-character defies the pressures and influences of his society by questioning the validity of the reality of which he is a part and by claiming that it is much like the fictions he himself creates and manipulates. He searches a world of literary imagination for radical solutions, learns that much of it is exhausted or elusive; lacking confidence in his enterprise, he nevertheless understands that his search is unending.

In Philip Roth's *The Counterlife* (1987) the novelist Nathan Zuckerman - a character largely indifferent to the possibilities of metafiction in the earlier

---

[*]Klinkowitz asserts that we deal here with "a deliberate parody of the Moebius strip style of fiction which obsessed Barth in his *Lost in the Funhouse* exercises." The point is arguable. Though Fenn Turner admits his attempt to write fiction twenty years earlier failed because the story was "bogged down in self-concern," he continues hoping his writing can be an ongoing affair. [Jerome Klinkowitz, *Literary Subversions*, p.15; John Barth, *Sabbatical*, p.36.]

Zuckerman Unbound, or *The Anatomy Lesson* - discovers the importance of confronting life as a literary construct. He states that literature, if used as a series of masks, disguises and changing roles, not only reveals reality's fictional alternatives but provides one with meaningful forms of "counterliving." "I can only exhibit myself in disguise. All my audacity derives from masks," he explains to another character in words that might serve as the novel's motto.[42] Zuckerman, going in the direction of Nabokov but avoiding authorial extremism, declares masks to be a natural expression of the human psyche. The so-called "being oneself" (revealing the writer's conscious self) is a naive illusion of the Western cultural tradition. The fear that being self-divided threatens mental health seems to him sadly erroneous. In fact, people who consciously, or unconsciously, invent reality's fictional alternatives, who impersonate "what they think they might like to be, believe they ought to be, or wish to be taken to be" are authentic and (paradoxically) whole.[43]

> All I can tell you with certainty is that I, for one, have no self, and that I am unwilling or unable to perpetrate upon myself the joke of a self....What I have instead is a variety of impersonations I can do...a troupe of players that I have internalized....But I certainly have no self independent of my imposturing, artistic efforts to have one. Nor would I want one. I am a theater and nothing more than a theater.[44]

According to Zuckerman, life is governed by stories, writers are controlled by fantasies, masks are inevitable. Writing is an on-going affair, a form of self-justification and self-renewal. The novelist pronounces his desire to track all these possibilities, to look for viable visions of reality. Roth's hero re-states what Sukenick, and Federman, Barth et al. have asserted, and his ability to mix imaginative exuberance, daring and humor with a convincing depiction of contemporary American life make his quest oddly persuasive and functional.

In *The Facts: A Novelist's Autobiography* (1988), which deceptively reads like a candid, realistically rendered autobiography of Roth, the text is preceded by a letter in which Roth asks his celebrated hero for advice and support. He confesses that he is "sick of fictionalizing" himself further, tired of the "masks, disguises, distortions and lies" embodied in the characters of his Portnoys, Kepeshes and Zuckermans.

> Is the book any good?...I've never worked before without my imagination being fired by someone like you or Portnoy or Tarnopol or Kepesh. I'm in no position to tell.[45]

In his response Zuckerman advises his creator that the book should not be published; its flaws are too obvious.

> Your acquaintance with the facts, your sense of the facts, is much less developed than your understanding of...fiction. You make a fictional world that is far more exciting than the world it comes out of...you no longer have any idea what *you* are or ever were. By now what you are is a walking text.[46]

By reviving his fictional hero in a book that he calls an autobiography Roth undercuts the validity of the material he is presenting. He also parodies the themes he put into his earlier work, including the concept of an alternate existence around which *The Counterlife* is built.

Transformations, so essential for Roth's characters, have always been accompanied by a need to question them, and, as a consequence, are often informed by new conflicts and dangers. Although ontological doubts and anxieties, which are characteristically foregrounded in metafiction, occur in his more traditional early work, these fundamental uncertainties form the subtext of Roth's current fascination with self-reflexive games. They torment Zuckerman, shadow his seemingly light-hearted involvements in metafiction. Masks and counterlives seriously complicate his relations with the outside world. He fears the possibility of being seen as "a terrorist," a maniac who is taking things "too far, 'tipping over the edge...like people who are on the edge of insanity,'" of being misunderstood and abandoned by his preferred partners in "counterliving."[47] Like Kafka,* Roth questions, with imagination and humor, his obsessive need to transcend himself as a writer, to make his artistic visions convincing, his fictions useful. He besets his writer-characters with doubts and fears that reflect a fragile but highly active and inventive writing self: a self torn between the isolation and boredom of creating texts and the extravagance of imagined possibilities, between exhaustion with literary tricks and the desire to engage in further transformations and fabulations. He imagines a self akin to Kafka's persona, one dedicated to an obsessive allegorized commitment to create literature that metamorphoses and renews itself through play, reduction, transmutation; but also through doubt, self-torment, even self-destruction.

The concern for artistic integrity which plagues characters in novels by Sukenick and Federman, Barth and Roth is balanced by their determination to keep their fictive processes alive, to deliver the various energies and possibilities contained in writing, to maintain the writer's position of importance and centrality. These writer-heroes typically manage to transcend the various crises they encounter, to emerge intact, to discover intense new creative possibilities and expanses of fiction, and to engage them with energy and devotion.

THE UNEASY COEXISTENCE

Imagining himself, in *Lost in the Funhouse*, as a future writer Ambrose dreams of nearly divine authorial power. He "envisions a truly astonishing funhouse,

---

*In *Deception*, Roth again turns to Kafka to redefine his perception of his literary idol. Philip meets, or imagines meeting, a former student who claims that "The Metamorphosis" and *The Trial* did not derive from Kafka's relationship with his father. It was the other way round, the student said. "By the time a novelist worth his salt is thirty-six, he's no longer translating experience into a fable - he's imposing his fable onto experience." Philip admires the wisdom of such a view. He, or the Roth for whom he speaks, no doubt remembers that in *The Professor of Desire*, Kepesh makes a point of defining Kafka's relation to reality differently. To Kepesh Kafka was a "fantasist" who transformed his everyday life into fable. [*Deception*, p.125.]

incredibly complex yet utterly controlled from a great central switchboard" and hopes he "could design such a place himself...be its operator."[48] In *Breakfast of Champions* the Vonnegut persona describes himself observing, "incognito," his own "fictional" characters: "I sat there in a cocktail lounge of my own invention, and I stared through my *leaks* at a white cocktail waitress of my own invention." The scene makes him feel he is "on a par with the Creator of the Universe."[49] "My every word's inverted, or reversed - or I am," says the authorial persona in Gass' *In the Heart of the Heart of the Country* and adds, "I held you, too, that way. You were so utterly provisional, subject to my change."[50]

Eager to assert authorial control within the world they describe, or imagine, writers in postmodernist fiction know well that whenever they want to be a part of it - and their very function requires that they *be* a part of it - they sooner or later have to deal with other figures that fill that world. Yet encounters and relationships between authors and the people around them are never simple. Postmodernist fiction is replete with conflicts between writers and their readers, friends, or family. Characters object to being treated badly, manipulated, misinformed, or cozened into submission by their authors. They resent having their secrets exposed, their privacy transgressed.*

The contention is not new to literature. The author-hero has always been, by the very nature of the role he plays in the text, in conflict with the world in which he lives, or describes. He has been the instrument of spiritual power and social influence, the person who can reveal lives and their secrets to the world. Yet confrontations between writers and other characters in the text, have rarely, until now, been dramatized so visibly. On the pages of recent American fiction they have become a source of new dramatic material, an exciting subject matter in itself.

Internal dissatisfaction with the writer in early postmodernist fiction takes the

---

*The novelist called R in Nabokov's *Transparent Things* (1972) refuses to "alter certain much too recognizable people" in the typescript of his new novel because that would, he says, be "tantamount to destroying the living prototype." Even if an editor made the artist change a character, "its prototype would remain recognizable by the shape of the hole left in the texture of the tale." [*Transparent Things* (Greenwich, Connecticut: Fawcett, 1974), pp.108-109.]

form of crude and straightforward attacks on him. Steve Katz is thus censured and challenged in his own text, *The Exaggerations of Peter Prince* (1968): "Where's the story? How are you going to catch us up in it and write a novel so the reader won't be able to put it down, he's so involved.... What will your friends say? They'll say, 'Katz, cut it out, you're making it all up. You're fucking around with boredom in our heads.'"[51]

Bernie, a would-be writer, one of the characters in Sukenick's *Up*, thus downgrades the book in progress, the material of *Up* itself:

> Between crisis and catastrophe who cares about your ego? Your complaint, your indignation, your outrage - your boils, your hangnails, your stomach pains. It turns to self-pity. This just bores us, we have the same problems. You ought to stick to comedy.[52]

The Death of the Novel and Other Stories offers a more imaginative example of friction between the author and his human environment. When the Sukenick persona asks his wife whether she minds being in the story in the company of other girls, she wants to know whether he does "lecherous things" with them. He answers: "No, I just fuck them." Pleased with himself, he muses:

> What I need is a bunch of friends who would be willing to become my characters for a whole story. Maybe I can hire some. Somebody ought to start a character rental service.[53]

Vonnegut's *Slaughterhouse-Five* contains another example of a sophisticated verbal showdown between a writer and a character he meets. Asked by a woman at a party if he will write about her, "in a book sometime," writer Kilgore Trout answers in the affirmative, then adds:

> And I'm not the only one who's listening. God is listening, too. And on

Judgement Day he's going to tell you all the things you said and did. If it turns out they're bad things instead of good things, that's too bad for you, because you'll burn forever and ever. The burning never stops hurting.[54]

Trout laughs when he sees that the woman "believed *that*, too," believed he was on par with God, a divine controller of humanity's conduct, the author of judgment.

In later American metafiction, characters' attacks on authors, and authors' reactions to them, are increasingly foregrounded, lively and intricate. Declared on various levels of expression, they are metaphorically suggestive and ontologically tangled. Gilbert Sorrentino makes it imaginable, in fact, on some level of metafictional make-believe strangely realistic, that disgruntled characters can take up an active struggle against those who create them. In *Mulligan Stew* (1979), a novel that is a spectacularly self-conscious, ingenious and rich example of writing about writing, characters are angered when they realize they are a part of a "grossly vulgar 'life'" created for them by one Tony Lamont, an avant-garde novelist. Convinced that Lamont is an inferior writer involved in endless increasingly paranoid disputes with critics and publishers, they begin to find ways of freeing themselves from his control. They "shift and blur" and say and do things that he finds confusing.[55] They understand that they can do it only by taking advantage of the technical complexities Lamont introduces but is not quite able to manage: "Had he told the story straightforwardly, we would have had no possibility of leaving him."[56] Halpin, one of the rebels, feels he has the right to be disobedient. He has been taken by Lamont from James Joyce's "vast construction," a work in which he was "used...fairly and with kindness." Other characters, like Daisy Buchanan, also have remarkable pedigrees and memories from "earlier jobs," and consequently cherish ambitions which are bound to be hurt by the inadequate circumstances and conditions of Lamont's novelistic construct.[57]

Once they learn that there is freedom outside of their allotted lives, Lamont's literary figures secretly communicate with each other, also with characters from other books, discuss the pleasures and risks of escaping the plot while their master is not working; wistfully they dream of walking out into the real world, "whatever kind of world it may be."[58] They conspire to reorganize the narrative by temporarily refusing to participate in it, or to abandon it altogether and join a colony of similarly disgruntled characters. They predict that authors "returning to work and not finding an important character are often forced to digress in an insane or ludicrous way," or that they engage in "boring and philosophical asides, ruminatory interludes, and endless descriptions of nature."[59]

The inhabitants of the author's fictive world, while arguing for an existence of their own, are as confused and frustrated, Sorrentino suggests, as those who create them. They are inconvenienced by the uncertain nature of their existence, tormented by ambition and competition, frightened by changes of market fashions or publisher's demands. Halpin's grievance passed on to a fellow-character is an echo of the novelist's dilemma:

> It was better to remain sensitive and open to decent, intelligent jobs than to get a reputation as a drudge who would work *anywhere as anything*. While authors distrust characters who run out on novels in progress, they respect them if the novels are garbage. The character who stays, to the bitter end, in a rotten book, dooms himself to a career of working in the same kind of book over and over again.[60]

As if to eliminate possible character defiance, Philip, the writer-hero in Roth's *Deception* (1990), denies his creations, including his wife, the right to be real. They are merely notebook jottings, he just imagines them, or imagines himself imagining them. And he himself is not quite what these characters take him for:

> ...its play, it is an *impersonation* of myself! Me *ventriloquizing* myself. Or maybe it's more easily grasped the other way around - everything here is falsified *except* me. Maybe it's *both*. But both ways or either way, what is

adds up to honey, is *homo ludens!*[61]

"The notebook jottings" try to protest, to prove their factuality, but seeing that the novelist is always in control, a trickster who can perpetually manipulate their lives, they feel defeated.

In Federman's *The Voice in the Closet* (1979) it is the writing itself that rebels. The voice of a twelve-year-old Jewish boy hidden in the closet while German soldiers arrest his family speaks to a writer called "federman," or "featherman," or "hombre della pluma," who tries, but fails, to write about the boy's survival. It wants the writer to tell the truth at last, to invalidate his earlier attempts (in *Double or Nothing* and *Take It or Leave It*), to capture his life by fiction. It also declares a desire to become a serious narrating presence, to develop an authentic narrative self. Such a self begins to emanate from the typewriter.[*] It would like to free itself of federman's language, memory and imagination, to be a free entity - "you federman with your noodles gambling my life away double or nothing in your verbal delirium" - but knows it may not be possible.[62] Even if "federman" died, the voice would face silence, a blank, it would "remain suspended from his blood lifeless voice within voice without a story."[63] Being a part of him, it participates in false interpretations, in blurring the truth.

In Vonnegut's *Breakfast of Champions* (1973) the conflict between writer and hero takes an unexpected turn. The Vonnegut persona criticizes himself for the abuse of the characters he creates. Central among them is Kilgore Trout, a science-fiction writer. Feeling ignored by readers and cheated and humiliated by publishers (his science-fiction stories are marketed in hard-core porno publications), Trout decides to subvert his own society. He does so by putting "bad ideas" into his books.[64]

---

[*]Reflecting on the degrees of reality within the various worlds established by postmodernist authors, Brian McHale sees the act of writing as "the one irreducible real reality." Having said that, however, the critic feels the ultimate in the metafictional "real" does not end here: "The harder we look for it, the more elusive and mirage-like it becomes...behind the reality of the writing must lie the superior reality of the *act* of writing that has produced it!" Federman is clearly fascinated with what else may lie behind the various Federman images and voices. [Brian McHale, *Postmodernist Fiction*, p.198.]

Invited one day to attend an Arts Festival, he plans to "embarrass the Festival to death" and to present himself as being "treated like a cockroach."[65] The showdown does indeed take place. Dwayne Hoover, a successful but unstable car dealer, having read Trout's novel, runs amok and injures a number of people, including Vonnegut. Trout is astonished at his own power: "*he* could bring evil into the world - in the form of bad ideas." Transformed by the experience, he now becomes "a fanatic on the importance of ideas and cures for diseases," a doctor of human minds, a "pioneer in the field of mental health."[66] A few years later he will receive the Nobel Prize for Medicine.*

Witnessing his hero's change of attitude, finding the Festival to be a mind-altering event, the Vonnegut persona is also spiritually "reborn." He realizes that "there was nothing sacred about myself or about any human being, that we were all machines, doomed to collide and collide and collide"; he also comes to understand that he wrote about these collisions like a machine.[67] Willing to accept moral responsibility as a writer, since Trout, his creation, functioned as a model for evil, Vonnegut apologizes to the astonished and suspicious Trout for damaging his mind, for not letting him feel a "wholeness and an inner harmony." He tells his character that he sets him at liberty, as "Count Tolstoy freed his serfs" and "Thomas Jefferson freed his slaves."[68] **

Roth's *The Facts* offers an equally imaginative author-hero confrontation. In the Prologue he, "Roth," requests that Zuckerman read and comment on the autobiographical contents of *The Facts*. Zuckerman is glad to oblige. He questions Roth's decisions, accuses him of falsifying life and engaging in "fiction-making tricks," points out that literary forthrightness is not simply the matter of intention:

---

*The writer-hero's decision to become a medical doctor so that he can better heal human souls recurs in several other prominent novels of the period, for example, in Roth's *The Anatomy Lesson* and Bellow's *Henderson the Rain King*. If this decision reflects, metaphorically, writers' yearnings, we have to remember that literary history records escape in the opposite direction. Prominent novelists like Conan Doyle, Walker Percy and, more recently, Michael Crichton, had in the past been physicians who abandoned their profession to be more effective and imaginative as writers.

**Vonnegut, the author of *Breakfast of Champions*, reneges on the promise the Vonnegut persona makes in the novel. Kilgore Trout reappears in *Jailbird* (1979).

...the distortion called fidelity is *not* your métier - you are simply too real to outface full disclosure. It's through *dis*simulation that you find your freedom from the falsifying requisites of 'candor.'

By raising Zuckerman's ontological status, Roth allows him to participate in "separating the facts from the imagination and emptying them of their potential dramatic energy," also in disputing the integrity of both himself and his literary character.[69]

But such enactments of authorial expiation, or self-criticism, are not usual in American fiction. Writer-heroes prefer to show themselves as victims of other people's wrath, envy, distrust. In *The Counterlife*, Zuckerman's brother is irate over Nathan's literary perfidy, his "using me to conceal himself while simultaneously disguising himself *as* himself, as *responsible*, as *sane*...." Such art is to him:

...an outright lie or a ridiculous travesty of the facts...everything important distorted, disguised, wrenched ridiculously out of proportion, determined by those endless, calculated illusions cunningly cooked up in this terrible solitude, everything self-calculation, deliberate deception....[70]

Reproaching Zuckerman for being both too sensitive and too radical about things Jewish, for acting as a "wild nut," Maria, his lover and later wife, points out how the novelist's obsession with anti-Semitism is a part of his love of conflict in general. And a part of his vocation:

You may have had your fill of fighting Jews and fighting fathers and fighting literary inquisitors - the harder you fight that sort of local opposition, the more your inner conflict grows....To be resisted, to be caught, to find yourself in the midst of a battle puts a spring in your heel. You're dying...for a collision, a clash - anything as long as there's enough antagonism to get the story smoking and everything exploding in the wrathful philippics you adore....You actually *like* to take things hard. You can't weave your stories otherwise.[71]

When Garp, in John Irving's *The World According to Garp* (1978), writes a novel about two couples involved in a sexual "foursome," his wife, Helen, feels that the book depicts her and Garp's relationship with their friends, the Fletchers, and is "an invasion of her privacy." "People *think* it's me, they *think* it's you. And sometimes I think so, too."[72] When Garp explains that there are differences between his fictive characters and the people of the real world, she brings up an argument that defines well the tension the metafictional writer aims at:

You have your own terms for what's fiction, and what's fact, but do you think other people know your system?[73]

Operating on another level of literary seriousness and artistic responsibility, Tim O'Brien describes, in *The Things They Carried* (1990), how a story his war buddy in Vietnam told him led to a controversy. Norman Bowker failed to save a friend when under attack and the two men virtually sank in the mixture of rain, mud and human feces. O'Brien, at Norman's request, changed liberally the scenery of the story and eliminated some key situations, "replacing this material with events that better fit the book's narrative." Feeling he failed to capture the drama of that event, "the terrible killing power of that shit field," he removed the story from the novel. Reworked and published in an anthology, the story was sent to Norman, whose reaction was "short and somewhat bitter": "you left out Vietnam," he wrote, "Where's Kiowa? Where's the shit?" The O'Brien persona explains that Bowker hanged himself eight months later. He decides to include the now "substantially revised" story in *The Things They Carried*, and to restore Norman Bowker's "real" name.[74]

Writer-heroes enjoy tales of how they manipulate, counterfeit or misrepresent other people's lives. They act surprised to learn characters have the ability to oppose them, to see through their tactics, to go beyond their assigned roles and consciousness. They flaunt the ease with which they deal with such dissentions. The dramatic structure and viability of the world they establish depends on such acts. Arguing with those who try to break out of narratives, or who question or resist the writer's authority gives them energy and strength. So does showing that there are no limits to their power to construct new, more enticing, more "real" human relationships or visions of life.

Yet, in confronting and controlling their human environment, postmodernist writer-heroes insist that their lives, so closely linked with fiction, cannot be expected to be easy or amicable because modern fiction challenges, provokes and confronts people's privacy, calls their world into question, imagines life according to the writers' own needs and assumptions. Aware of the postmodernist writer's deep-rooted need to subvert received concepts of reality, to annoy or provoke his audience, one of the characters of *The Counterlife* points out to Zuckerman:

> But tranquillity is disquieting to you, Nathan, in writing particularly - it's bad art to you, far too comfortable for the reader and certainly for yourself. The last thing you want is to make readers happy....[75]

"REAL" AUTHOR AS HERO

Clearly, the mainstream postmodernist novelist has an obsessive need to confront the insubordinate material of fiction under his own name. American fiction of recent decades features characters that conspicuously call themselves Sukenick, Federman, Katz, Vonnegut, Mailer, Exley, Barth, Didion, Tim O'Brien, Roth.

Authors have inscribed themselves into novels since the early stages of the genre, but the practice of breaking in upon the fictional world has been pursued by postmodernists so frequently and determinedly, with such sense of variance and imagination, that we can regard it as a major and representative development in writer-hero fiction. This vogue gives fiction the sense of a uniquely forefronted and revitalized authorial presence. Jerome Klinkowitz calls it "the most radical of disruptive literary techniques, the presence of a self-conscious writer within his story."[76]

Personal idiosyncrasies and diversity of imagination and style provide this supposedly real-life author fiction with a rich and varied gallery of self-portraits. They emphasize the importance of fiction's shifting levels of consciousness and highlight the tensions between fabulation and actuality, between autobiography and fictionalized biography. The apparently factual in this "transworld identity" of the self-conscious writer clashes with the obviously fictive.[77] One distinguishes the hero's self and the author's self (even if the two are reflections of each other, that is, when the names and lives of the hero *in* the work and author *of* the work coincide), the self of the protagonist that a fictional hero invents and the self of that hero, the two above selves and the author that creates them. Fictional writer-heroes and real-life authors, outer and inner selves, life and art become reflected, twinned, multiplied, contrasted, but also peculiarly unified, just as supposedly outer and inner narratives are unified.

The reader, the receiving end of this confrontational drama, is left to wonder about the plausibility of the hero's personal-spatio-temporal contiguities, to speculate if he deals with the authentic Barth, Roth, or Vonnegut, if these authors have really done or said in the real-world what they do and say as characters in the text. If he questions the validity and relevance of tales that are often called "real stories" or "real autobiographies," he unwittingly plays the role which he has been assigned: co-creator of the narrating self.[*]

Ways in which real-life writers enter their texts vary. Some factually coincide with real-world authors, or make allusions to them but their names are changed,

---

[*]"Modern autobiography is indeed a Hall of Mirrors," points out Marjorie Smelstore. Its authors not only "believe in life as process...but, more significantly...they are committed to the unfinished quality of the selves, both their authorial and autobiographical selves." [Marjorie Smelstore, "A Hall of Mirrors: Modern Autobiography and the Process of Creating the Self," *Prose Studies*, London, December 1984, Vol.7, #3, p.240.]

disguised or camouflaged. Nabokov's heroes, for example, use abbreviations or anagrams like V, Vivian Darkbloom, Vadim Vadimovitch, etc. thereby making innumerable references to, or identifying themselves with, their author. For example, at the end of *Pale Fire* (1962), Charles Kinbote, when asked about his future declares he will "continue to exist" under "other disguises," possibly as "an old, happy, healthy, heterosexual Russian, a writer in exile, sans fame, sans future, sans audience, sans anything but his art."[78]

Nathan Zuckerman's life, as depicted in Philip Roth's *Zuckerman Unbound*, as well as in other "Zuckerman" novels, frequently resembles Roth's biography. He was born in Newark in 1933. His first bestseller, the scandalous and erotic "Carnovsky," was published, like *Portnoy's Complaint*, in 1969. His conflicts with Jewish readers and critics resemble Roth's problems in the early sixties. In several recent novels by Roth characters called "Philip," or "Roth" similarly accommodate facts and situations strikingly resembling elements of real-life Roth's own biography. Parallels include the pilgrimages to Kafka's birthplace and the meetings with the Czechoslovak dissidents, the visits to Israel and England.

Paul Theroux persistently evokes in fiction circumstances pertaining to his own life and work. In *My Secret History* (1989), for example, Andre Parent is an American novelist who lived in Africa and the Far East, who is settled in London, and who achieved fame as a travel-writer. Theroux' note at the beginning of the novel that "the characters all strolled out of my imagination" should be seen, Wendy Steiner points out, as yet another "post-modern tease of 'this is really me, but I, like everyone, am a fiction.'"[79]

As another ploy, indirect and unobtrusive, the author may act as editor of the text supposedly written by another writer. Or he may be addressed, in a preface, by his hero. In *Mother Night*, for example, Vonnegut poses as editor of "the confessions of Howard W. Campbell, Jr." - which is the text of *Mother Night*. He tells us Campbell was not only a person accused of "extremely serious crimes," but also a liar, yet does not explain what is false or authentic in the text. This is in line with the view Vonnegut "risks" in his editorial note: "lies told for the sake of artistic effect...can be, in a higher sense, the most beguiling forms of truth."[80]

In Updike's *Bech: A Book*, Bech writes in the Forward: "Dear John...if you must commit the artistic indecency of writing about a writer, better I suppose about me than about you." He recognizes himself as being more like Mailer, or Bellow than the "stolid old homely yours truly," points to all kinds of shortcomings, suggests some changes, but finds his fictional representation essentially accurate and useful.[81]

Sorrentino calls attention to himself in *Mulligan Stew* in a more direct way. He precedes the novel with letters from editors and publishers who negatively assessed *Mulligan Stew*. He thus puts himself beside his hero, Lamont, an untalented novelist involved in a dispute with critics and publishers. While acting on different ontological planes, the two authors denounce and parody the conventions of writing and publishing in America.

Still another ontologically confusing and structurally disruptive way of authorial penetration of the text occurs when the real-world author appears in it briefly, like a guest. Kurt Vonnegut makes a momentary appearance in *Slaughterhouse-Five*, when his protagonist, Billy Pilgrim, a prisoner-of-war in Nazi Germany, visits the latrine. Sick with diarrhoea, fearing he is excreting "his brains," aware that Billy does not know him, Vonnegut says: "That was I. That was me. That was the author of this book."[82]

In *Up*, Sukenick not only appears as Sukenick, but makes it known that it is possible for other writers, similarly present in their own texts, to visit him there. While addressing guests at a party celebrating the completion of *Up*, he recognizes Steve Katz, "briefly on a special guest appearance from his own novel."[83] Steve Katz, while inside his own *The Exaggerations of Peter Prince*, not only returns the kindness of mentioning Sukenick but explains that appearing in *Up* delayed his own narrative.

The illusionist bravura with which these narrators speak of the facility with which they move across boundaries of imagination and possibility is typically shadowed by a sense of uncertainty and nervousness which so often mars the

64

existence of the metafictional hero. The narrator of *Take It or Leave It* who, like Katz, briefly leaves his own narrative "post," thus excuses himself: "Oh you guys want to know where I was? Why I left my post...why I deserted my recitation? Deserted! You guys exaggerate. I had to go to the bathroom. No...I'm kidding. I went to see a friend. Buddy of mine, Ronnie. Ronald Sukenick....He was having problems with his story. Wanted me to help a bit. I was only gone a short time."[84]

Longer, more sustained and foregrounded appearances of writers in their own fictional plots indicate the importance of this admixture of authorial bravado/anxiety in postmodernist texts. Vonnegut's presence in *Breakfast of Champions*, for example, suffuses the novel with an aura of oppressive bafflement and comical ambiguity. Calling himself Vonnegut, alluding to a number of his own personal experiences and biographical data, he shows himself as both a shrewd ruler of his fictive world and a person who is inane and absurd, gaudy and ostentatious, a slapstick figure.[*] He claims he is faced with an emotional and artistic crisis, admits he is crude - he makes his living "by being impolite" - that the book he is writing is "very bad."[85] But his sorrows and complaints, at one point bleak and tortured, are later denied or ignored. The text, illustrated with dozens of Vonnegut's (or "Vonnegut's") own crude, childlike drawings, is also equipped with apparently factual details of Vonnegut's own life. For example, he divulges the length of his penis. While thus caricaturing himself, the Vonnegut persona frequently intimates that under the layers of stupor and irony he dreams of a regained state of authority and innocence, of leaving his own instability and timidity, and of moving on to a new, more stable and pleasant realm of awareness.

Joan Didion inserts herself into her *Democracy* in a more urbane way. She announces her appearance in the novel in a provisional manner (an allusion to Melville) but suggests that she is going to act as a factual and unassuming character:

---

[*]At the beginning of *Slapstick: Lonesome No More* (1976), Vonnegut explains that the old "slapstick film comedies" are like "what life *feels* like" to him. [*Slapstick: Lonesome No More* (New York: Delacorte, 1976), p.1]

Call me the author.

Let the reader be introduced to Joan Didion, upon whose character and
doings much will depend of whatever interest these pages may have, as she
sits at her writing table in her own room in her own house on Welbeck
Street.[86]

Didion never quite introduces herself, nor is she instrumental in the course of the
novel as she promises. She withdraws from the events of the story, reduces herself
to a curious and perplexed background observer forever dazed and numbed by the
skeins and puzzles of the life she watches. Then she briefly brings herself to the
forefront, discusses her teaching at Berkeley, her changing perception of time. She
makes herself awkward rather than eloquent, hesitant rather than sagacious. It is not
the author's own life, she is suggesting, that should be central in the process of
assembling the world from its broken images. And yet, her presence as author-
persona is unmistakable; she is a perceptive, intelligent observer of events which
require reconstruction.

In Roth's novels complications ensue from the real-world writer's tortuous
correlations with his fictional image. Apparent similarities prove to be different,
analogies become ambiguities, facts become fictions. Characters who are
Zuckerman, Philip, or Roth instruct us that they are not Zuckerman, or Philip, or
Roth, that fiction is not "naked autobiography," but rather "mock-autobiography or
hypothetical autobiography or autobiography grandiosely enlarged."[87] In his recent
Operation Shylock, Roth again argues that the problems regarding the identity and
credibility of "Philip Roth" are his own, that he, rather than his double, is the victim
of living between facts and the fictionalizing imagination, between the written and
the unwritten world:

I knew all about these fictions about the fictions of the self-divided....But this
was no book I was studying or one I was writing, nor was this double a
character in anything other than the vernacular sense of that word....I was

being confounded by somebody who, very simply, was not me, who had nothing to do with me, who called himself by my name but had no relation to me.[88]

This mode of textual presence/absence becomes increasingly attractive for the writer-heroes of the 1980s. Kosinski appropriates the technique in his last novel, *The Hermit of 69th Street*, the story of Norbert Kosky, the famous and brilliant Polish émigré novelist, who purportedly gave the manuscript to Kosinski to annotate and edit. But Kosky is unmistakably similar to his editor. He was born in Lodz, Poland, a 54 year-old survivor of the Holocaust who emigrated to America, where he achieved fame and notoriety after writing several controversial but respected novels. Like Kosinski he has been accused of plagiarism.

Kosinski (J.K. or Jay Kay) regularly intervenes in Kosky's narrative, confusing identities and planes of existence. At one point, when Kosky asks Jay Kay for advice about what to write about, the latter instructs him: "Anything or anyone that you find particularly exciting or excitable." When the book is nearing completion, Kosky decides to disassociate himself from his mentor; he determines to change the title because "another writer is soon coming out with a novel called *The Hermit*." Asked who the other writer is, Kosky replies "Kosinski....That other Kosotoxin Kid."[89]

Such authorial penetration of the text is frequently accompanied by references to real-life authors' work.* Novelistic reflections of Kosinski, Roth, Vonnegut, Barth, et al. increasingly rely on what has been done and said by their creators in earlier fictions. Plots, heroes, situations and opinions are revived and used as if they were vital, self-contained and self-referential historical entities. Authors reduce their dependence on the outside world and look for inspiration to the world

---

*Rather than being an "entity," these author-characters reduce themselves to "function," or an "institution," Michel Foucault points out. Their aim is not to "re-establish the theme of an originating subject, but to grasp the subject's points of insertion, modes of functioning, and systems of dependencies." [Michel Foucault, "What is an author?" in Josue Harari, ed., *Textual Strategies: Perspectives in Post-Structuralist Criticism* (Ithaca, Cornell University Press, 1979), p.144.]

they have created. What some critics[*] see as a loss is regarded by American postmodernists as a rich source of energy and motivation.

Celebrating their past literary deeds and attitudes authors test the viability of their former and present attitudes, arrange their own trials, confront their doubts and fears. Their writing and their lives, self-reflexively interlaced, serve as material for revision and reinvention, as a motivation for a possible spiritual or artistic transformation, or as a source of psychic liberation. They undertake an effort to see viewpoints and selves up-dated, perpetually absorbed in the act of creation, turned into an on-going literary thriller. The novelist acting as his own hero does not merely focus on growth, Heide Ziegler observes, he "devises his own *Buildung* in retrospect" and thus, as if, doubles himself:

> ...by introducing himself as protagonist of his own text, the writer proposes a distance from his former self....This leads to an autobiographical paradox. There is a former self and a present self; and language has both to define and to relate them.[90]

John Barth's *LETTERS* (1979) is a pertinent example. In this epistolary novel, which is a highly-imaginative and parodic re-working of the genre, Barth resurrects the characters or their descendants who appear in his earlier novels in order to integrate them into the plot, a scheme of interrelationships that is overseen by one central character, the "Author" called Barth. Corresponding with them, interpreting their deeds, untangling their thoughts, justifying his own actions and decisions, he is Ambrose Mensch redux, the Operator, the man in control, a God-like creator no longer concealed or diffident; he is someone in whose "immodest and subversive

---

[*]Michiko Kakutani, for example, observes: "Few novelists today, after all, can draw upon the sort of adventures that a Conrad or Hemingway once had and so fall back increasingly on the details of their own lives as writers - lives that consist for the most part of sitting in a room, playing with words and sentences." Yet Kakutani's claim is narrowly selective. Few novelists (one thinks of Flaubert, James, Proust, Joyce, Kafka as counter examples) lived adventurous lives. [Michiko Kakutani, "The Hero as Writer," *New York Times Book Review*, July 11, 1982.]

resemblance to God," as Barth noted in an essay, one sees "a clue to our universe."[91] Cold, distant, never short of new imaginative fantasies or creative energy, he proudly flaunts and brilliantly executes the idea that a writer can find a sense of order and meaning in retrieving his previous statements, as if they were, as Frederick Karl puts it, his "computer retrieval systems," reviewing and re-cycling the stances contained in them, disputing and confronting the aesthetics and the conclusions he had once instilled with a sense of fictional finality.[92]

They, the artifacts of fiction, provide Barth-the-Author with material for comments and observations, but also with changes, evolutions and re-cyclings of earlier fictive situations. Ambrose Mensch (of *Lost in the Funhouse*), now an avant-garde writer and university professor, has a love affair with Lady Amherst and claims he is relost in the funhouse. Todd Andrews, almost seventy-years-old, alters the events that took place in *The Floating Opera* and reverses the concepts he held in that novel. His new motto is "EVERYTHING has intrinsic value."[93] A.B. Cook, a descendant of the son of Ebenezer Cooke's sister and Henry Burlingame of *The Sot-Weed Factor*, tries to bring coherence to the tortuous history of his ancestry, but his evaluation of the various strands of American history only generates "intrigues and counter intrigues," all confusing and questionable, open to new uses and interpretations. Jerome Bray, a literary progeny of the fictional Harold Bray from *Giles Goat-Boy* and consequently a character who is uncertain whether he is real or fictional, tries to use a giant computer to create a pure, futuristic form of communication: a computerized digital "Revolutionary Novel" in which there is no message or other meaning-carrying devices.

These revised characters of *LETTERS*, when compared with their prototypes, are no longer cardboard figures arranged and shuffled by their author, but appear as recognizable denizens of contemporary America. They are more involved in present-day issues, and they display a greater measure of optimism and affirmation of life. Without deviating largely from the formal experimentation of metafiction, Barth-the-Author assigns the characters of *LETTERS* a large measure of authority and human compassion. And he, as "Barth," is a more sustained and convincing author-figure as compared to his earlier protagonists.[*]

Inscribed authors engage in yet another widely-practiced postmodernist technique: they use the occasion to refer to real-world authors, politicians or critics, as if they existed on the same level of ontological possibility. These "textual authors" analyze, compliment or, more frequently, reproach well-known personages. References may include off-hand, lighthearted jabs aimed at fellow-novelists or their work. Vonnegut thus briefly mentions Mailer in *Slaughterhouse-Five*:

> One of them said that it would be a nice time to bury the novel....Another one said that people couldn't read well enough anymore to turn print into exciting situations in their skulls, so that authors had to do what Norman Mailer did, which was to perform in public what he had written.[94]

Often personal scores are settled in print. The reader is witness to quarrels with other writers, critics, or publishers about their work, sometimes the novel he/she is presently reading. Philip Roth is famous for his thinly-fictionalized attacks on his critics. In *Operation Shylock* the author is thus comforted by his admiring double:

> The insults you've put up with, they drive me nuts on your behalf. *Portnoy's Complaint*, not even nominated for a National Book Award!...Podhoretz - I actually cannot speak the man's name without tasting gall in my mouth. And Gilman - that attack on *When She Was Good*, on the integrity of *that book*....And Professor Epstein, *there's* a genius. And those broads at *Ms.* And this exhibitionist Wolcott -"[95]

Mailer's confrontation with America's "liberal academic intelligentsia," in *The*

---

[*]In Barth's most recent work, *Once Upon a Time* (1994), the central character, John Barth, is a successful novelist who has just turned sixty. The novel is a contrived mixture of reflexive images, memories of his own life and literary career, echoes from his earlier books, revelations and anecdotes, also his "counterself." Yet, as in LETTERS, Barth is not recounting his life but "a story" of it.

Armies of the Night, is all the more intense because the Mailer persona engages his adversaries within the novel. A group of American intellectuals is attacked for being fooled by cheap utopian visions of progress and lacking the insight and vitality Americans need to deal with the confusions of the new age. While officially opposed to the tactics of the government, these conformists actually help "to convert the citizenry to a plastic mass." Mailer describes Robert Lowell, the chief representative of these "servants of the moon" and collaborators with "technology land" as "a reclining shepherd contemplating his flute," an artist whose WASP mentality and genteel sensitivity may find the "*mess*" of the current situation "finally too shapeless."[96]

In *The Hermit of 69th Street*, the Kosky/Kosinski character fiercely refutes the accusation of plagiarism, clearly an echo of the 1982 *Village Voice* charge. He mercilessly lampoons his accusers, attacks the media for the love of fabrications, and the society for feeding on scandal and for believing that lie-detectors are reliable.

In *Music for Chameleons* (1980) Truman Capote catalogues literary personalities he hates. Robert Frost, "an evil, selfish bastard," "an egomaniacal double-crossing sadist" who "wrecked his whole family," is one of them. Ernest Hemingway is similarly "a really dishonest man, the closet-everything." Thomas Wolfe is "that purple upchuck." Capote then justifies himself in a lame manner: "Ah, well, hm, let's see: how difficult, the rivalry factor being what it is, for one contemporary author, or would-be author, to confess admiration for another."[97]

In renouncing traditional barriers between biography and fiction these literary look-alikes find, as if unexpectedly, a source of new artistic excitement. They oscillate between the celebration of the creative self and self-mocking inquiry, between acting as manipulators of life and falling victim to their own imagination, between aiming, however ironically, at moral seriousness and mocking value systems. Sukenick's dictum in *The Death of the Novel*, "We must divest ourselves of all mechanical response, get rid of our habits....We improvise our novels as we improvise our lives," remains an insightful, richly varied and colorfully-documented characteristic of the American novelist of the last few decades.[98]

A HEALTHY DOSE OF REALISM

William Gass, in discussing his concern that "serious writing" should be produced "for the sake of the art," admits he cannot help being suspicious of his own "detachment" from realism.[99] His readers share the sentiment. One critic wrote that his stories are "informed with a realist's passion for detail of experience" and that his unnamed narrator in *In the Heart of the Heart of the Country* is an obvious shadow of Gass himself. Another critic laments: "How autobiographical it might be if autobiographical fiction were possible!"[100]

But *In the Heart of the Heart of the Country* was published in 1968, when, in spite of doubts and counterclaims, metafictionists make fervent declarations of fidelity to disruptive, non-representational and radically self-conscious literary forms. Several years later the divide between those who see the novel as a form striving to replace mimetic realism, and those who believe that experience does not translate itself into the language of stylistic and formal virtuosity narrows. In practice, a good deal of self-reflexive fiction goes, with amazing zest and flexibility, in the direction of realism. Even avowed believers in the hegemony of metafictional prose admit that abandoning realism is somehow impossible. They accept that adding relevance, conventional characterization, and description to illusory or surreal images is an effective way to stress fantasy, fragmentation or discontinuity. For many, realism becomes the synthesizing element that binds the diversities and tensions of metafiction.

As we move closer to the 1980s the term "reality" is seen as being largely ambiguous or irrelevant. Two decades of postmodernist attitudes dilute rigorous mimetic practices. At the same time critics like John Gardner and Gerald Graff point out that officially and commercially promoted *unreality* is often proposed as *reality*, that postmodernist fiction instead of resisting such pragmatic stances imitates them and thus becomes indistinguishable from official affectation. Consequently, Graff points out, "In a paradoxical and fugitive way, mimetic theory remains alive.

Literature holds the mirror up to unreality....But "unreality" in this sense is not a fiction but the element in which we live."[101]

Writer-heroes of recent fiction draw energy from such disputes. They willingly engage in commentaries on the importance of repossessing reality, of mixing it with illusionary worlds, of penetrating both and moving freely from one to the other. In a letter to Todd Andrews, in *LETTERS*, Barth-the-Author declares: "I approach reality these days with more respect, if only because I find it less realistic and more mysterious than I'd supposed."[102] In *Sabbatical* and the later, thematically related, *The Tidewater Tales* (1987) and *The Last Voyage of Somebody the Sailor* (1991), characters speak of their interest in the socio-political realities of America and realistic representation of life.

In *Sabbatical* the Turners agree on the importance of re-adopting realism in the novel they are writing, but insist on giving it a more contemporary meaning. They envision a mixture of the factual, the romantic, the mysterious and the fantastic, a formula they call "the Truly Irreal" or "the Literary Marvelous."

> The literary marvelous is what we want, with a healthy dose of realism to keep it ballasted....Realism is your keel and ballast of your effing ship and story, and a good plot is your mast and sails. But magic is your wind, Suse. Your literary marvelous is your mother-effing wind.[103]

Searching for the "literary marvelous," the protagonists of *Sabbatical* attempt to escape both the tedium of life, which they link with traditional realism, and what they see as the paralyzing formal rigidity and suffocating mentality of the current postwar novel. Their sea voyage, besides being a sabbatical and an adventure, is an expedition against the currents of modern literary dogmas, a search for new winds of word and thought. What they find in the waters of "occidental fiction" since "circa 1960" is pathetically used-up, ailing and stagnant:

> ...the Beat Generation has degenerated, the Existentialists no longer exist, the

French New Novelists have grown old, the Angry Young Men are middle-aged and petulant, the Black Humorists are serious and tenured, the Jews are assimilated, the Latinos are lively and expatriated, the blacks and redskins pale by comparison, the homosexuals are still clearing their throats, the new feminists aren't impressive though numerous women are, Master Nabokov is dead, Master Beckett is silent, Master Borges has turned into Rudyard Kipling, the Nobel prize is being awarded like Swedish foreign aid to obscure authors whom even smart Susan has scarcely heard of and who evidently lose everything but their kroners in translation, there's something called Postmodernism, and, so, so it seems to our Fenn, lots of room at the top in the decade ahead.[104]

The Turners, like Barth's earlier artists, believe that writing is more important than the writer, that their individuality and authority are being asserted in the act of writing and in the continuity of fiction-making, not in the complexities of socio-political environment, but they also want writing to be a more relevant tool in dealing with the affairs of daily life, their professions, their families, the state of their country. Adjusting to his heroes' growing interest in realism, Barth renders the surfaces of their lives with remarkably meticulous verisimilitude.

While Barth and other metafictionists shift towards the freer, more imaginative use of realism, a counter movement is taking place. Writers who for years embodied the realistic tradition now want to add to it the potency of postmodernist illusion-making. They discover that mimetic and metafictional modes, when mingled, or played against each other, can lead to new and surprisingly effective results in which the meaning of representational writing is not only unsubverted, but can actually be enriched, or given an interesting sense of perspective - especially when dealing with the complexities of writing and a writer's inner life.

Philip Roth is a late convert to metafiction. Having established himself as a novelist in the tradition of realistic narration and description, he signals, in the 1970s, a growing interest in linking reality and fantasy. He also explores the view that the contemporary novelist is psychologically and aesthetically indebted to both. In *My Life as a Man* (1974), Tarnopol, a young ambitious writer confronted with the sudden death of a woman who for several years made his life miserable, engages in a monologue in which he is embarrassed and stupefied by the unreality of American reality:*

> Defies credulity. If in a work of realistic fiction the hero was saved by something as fortuitous as the sudden death of his worst enemy, what intelligent reader would suspend his disbelief? Facile, he would grumble, and fantastic. Fictional wish fulfillment, fiction in the service of one's dreams. Not True to Life. And I would agree. Maureen's death is not True to Life.[105]

In other Roth fictions, heroes are increasingly attracted to roles in which they confront, or imitate, what they see as reality's improbabilities and deceptions. In "'I Always Wanted You to Admire my Fasting'; or Looking at Kafka" (1973), he imagines that Kafka did not die of tuberculosis in 1924, but survived the war and emigrated to America, where he worked as a teacher of Hebrew. Fantasy is given a self-reflexive twist. The nine-year-old Roth is one of Kafka's students. When at the end of the story Kafka dies at the age of seventy, leaving no survivors or books, Roth-the-character, is fifteen and "trying to write short stories."[106] In *The Breast* (1972), having turned into a female breast, Kepesh reminds us throughout that he was shaped by writers like Gogol and Kafka, authors gifted with the ability, he says, to "envision the incredible" and grasp "the extreme in literature." His own metamorphosis confuses him greatly. Yet, he rationalizes proudly that, as one who not only "imagines the marvelous transformation," but in fact "marvelously

---

*In "Writing American Fiction" - originally a speech (1960) - Roth states: "the actuality is continually outdoing our talents, and the culture tosses up figures almost daily that are the envy of any novelist." [*Reading Myself and Others* (New York: Farrar, Straus and Giroux, 1975), p.120.]

transforms himself," he has "out-Kafkaed Kafka," become "the greater artist."[107] In *The Ghost Writer* (1979), Zuckerman, the fledgling author of four published short stories fantasizes about the power of imagination -- "if only I could invent as presumptuously as real life!" -- of being a part of the unrestrained world of love and sex. When he meets Amy, a daunting young woman, he takes her for Anne Frank, who has miraculously survived Auschwitz, imagines himself marrying her, calls her "this impassioned little sister of Kafka's, his lost little daughter....everything he dreamed in Prague was, to her, real Amsterdam life. What he invented, she suffered."[108]

These works reflect Roth's desire to act out fictions that can both rival the complexities and puzzles of life and symbolically annul the rigors of the Western literary heritage, reduce the accepted canons of artistic perception to unimaginative helplessness and replenish it with authorly inventiveness and imagination. In the 1980s and the early 1990s Roth engages - through his "front man," Zuckerman, and several Roth-like figures - in increasingly bizarre and quixotic self-reflexive constructs which suggest that writers' imaginative exuberance is offset by anguish and punishment.

Similarly, John Irving's *The World According to Garp* is a brilliant study of the relationship between biographical data and their transformation into fiction. Preparing himself to be a writer, Garp is aware that fiction cannot mirror life, since "the *worst* reason for anything being part of a novel is that it really happened. *Everything* has really happened, sometime!"; consequently, "Fiction has to be better made than life."[109] When his publisher cautions him that to most readers the idea of "improving upon reality is pure bunk" and points out that his new novel, called "The World According to Bensenhaver," is "...somehow, soap opera; it's too *much*, somehow," Garp self-assuredly replies: "*Life* is too much, somehow. *Life* is an X-rated soap opera...."[110] Soon he realizes that the "too much" of the outer life catches up with his own life. The book brings him wealth and fame, but his life becomes a string of bizarre tragedies. He learns that fiction writing is a difficult, baffling and recipe-resistant activity in which "everything seems to be related to everything else," and in which, as in cooking, "you can have all the right ingredients, give plenty of time and care, and still get nothing."[111]

In Capote's *Answered Prayers* (1987) the writer-figure remarks on the perversely elusive quality of terms like "truth" or "illusion":

> Because something is true doesn't mean that it's convincing, either in life or in art. Think of Proust. Would *Remembrance* have the ring that it does if he had made it historically literal, if he hadn't transposed sexes, altered events and identities? If he had been absolutely factual, it would have been less believable, but...better....That's the question: is truth an illusion, or is illusion truth, or are they essentially the same? Myself, I don't care what anybody says about me as long as it isn't true.[112]

A number of other American authors similarly discover that playing with the distinctions between mimesis and fabulation, reality and fantasy is a dynamic and effective means of writing about writers. Characters that emerge from their novels are noticeably different from those populating American fiction in earlier periods. Freed of the didactic elements and the social determinism of realistic/naturalistic modes or the rigid formality of early postmodernism, contemporary writers yearn for some final sense of reality existing somewhere between a life composed of the details and textures of late century America and imaginative fictitiousness, between public recognition and witty self-annulment.

To achieve such ends they repudiate the older concept of the artist, divest themselves of the old status and dignity, vow that the act of writing is no longer a special gift, a privileged activity. They insist that they cannot save, much less improve, the world, or deal with expanding forces of evil. Frequently, they are prepared to belittle or humiliate themselves, to reveal themselves as foolish eccentrics or clowns. These testimonies of incompetence and confusion notwithstanding, they are rather stubborn and serene operators of the funhouse of literary possibilities. Commenting on Zuckerman's adoption, "in middle age," of an intensely self-reflexive attitude, a female character in *The Counterlife* calls the novelist "a calmly detached observer, a bit more of a percipient spy on the agony of others, rather than, as of old, being tossed and torn apart."[113]

NOTES

1.Jerome Klinkowitz, *The Practice of Fiction in America: Writers from Hawthorne to the Present* (Ames: The Iowa State University Press, 1980), p.8.

2.Raymond Federman, "Self-Reflexive Fiction," in *Columbia Literary History of the United States*, Emory Elliott, ed., (New York: Columbia University Press, 1988), p.1154.

3.Barthelme, *Snow White* (New York: Athenaeum, 1977), p.18.

4.Barthelme, *Great Days* (New York: Farrar, Straus and Giroux, 1970), p.145, Henry James, "The Art of Fiction", in *Henry James: Essays on Literature* (New York: The Library of America, 1984), p.53.

5.Gilbert Sorrentino, *Splendide Hôtel* (1973, Elmwood Park: Dalkey Archive Press, 1984), p.25.

6.Ibid., pp.9-10.

7.James Simon Kunen, *The Strawberry Statement* (New York: Random House, 1969), p.7.

8.Ibid., p.6.

9.Richard Brautigan, *Trout Fishing in America, The Pill versus the Springhill Mine Disaster, and In Watermelon Sugar* (Boston: Houghton Miffin, 1989), pp.1, 4, 107, 9-10.

10.Donald Barthelme, *Snow White*, p.129.

11.David Lodge, *The Modes of Modern Writing* (London: Edward Arnold, 1977), p.226.

12.Gilbert Sorrentino, "The Various Isolated: W. C. Williams' Prose," *New American Review*, No.15 (1972), p. 196-97.

13.Ronald Sukenick, *Up* (New York: A Delta Book, 1970), p.222-23.

14.Raymond Federman, in "Self-Reflexive Fiction," *Columbia Literary History of the United States*, p.1155.

15.Ronald Sukenick, *Up*, p.217.

16.Ibid., p.210.

17.Ibid., p.329.

18.William H. Gass, *Willie Master's Lonesome Wife* (New York: Knopf, 1971), no page numbering.

19.Donald Barthelme, *Snow White*, pp.82-83.

20.Raymond Federman, *Take It or Leave It* (New York: Fiction Collective, 1976), chapter XV, no page numbering.

21.Ronald Sukenick, *The Death of the Novel and Other Stories* (New York: Dial Press, 1969), p.57.

22.Ronald Sukenick, *Out* (Chicago: Swallow, 1973), p.136.

23.Federman, Raymond, *Take It or Leave It*, chap.0, no page numbering.

24.Raymond Federman, *Double or Nothing* (Chicago: The Swallow Press, 1971), p.0.

25.Paul Auster, *The New York Trilogy* (1985, London, Boston: Faber and Faber, 1987), pp.130-31.

26.Ibid., pp. 313-14.

27.Ronald Sukenick, *The Death of the Novel and Other Stories*, p.41.

28.Ibid., p.53.

29.Paul Auster, *The New York Trilogy*, p. 296.

30.Philip Roth, *The Counterlife* (New York: Farrar, Straus, Giroux, 1986), p.321.

31.Joan Didion, *Democracy* (New York: Simon and Schuster, 1984), p.108-110.

32.Ibid., pp.29-30.

33.Ibid, p.232.

34.Ronald Sukenick, *The Death of the Novel and Other Stories*, pp.57, 49, 100.

35.John Barth, *Lost in the Funhouse* (1968; New York: Bantam, 1969), p.94.

36.Ibid., p.114.

37.Ibid., p.116.

38.John Barth, *Chimera*, pp.10-11.

39.Mary McCarthy, "A Bolt from the Blue", *The New Republic*, June 4, 1962.

40.Vladimir Nabokov, *Look at the Harlequins!* (New York: McGraw-Hill, 1974), pp.97, 85.

41.John Barth, *Sabbatical* (1982, London: Panther, Granada Publishing, 1984), p.301.

42.Philip Roth, *The Counterlife*, p.275.

43.Ibid., p.319.

44.Ibid., p.320-21.

45.Philip Roth, *The Facts* (1988; New York: Penguin, 1989), pp.6, 10.

46.Ibid., p.162.

47.Philip Roth, *The Counterlife*, p.321.

48.John Barth, *Lost in the Funhouse*, p.93.

49.Kurt Vonnegut, *Breakfast of Champions*, pp.192-200.

50.William H. Gass, *In the Heart of the Heart of the Country* (1968; Boston: David R. Godine, 1981), p.196.

51.Steve Katz, *The Exaggerations of Peter Prince* (New York: Holt, Rinehart and Winston, 1968), p.3.

52.Ronald Sukenick, *Up*, p.56.

53.Ronald Sukenick, *The Death of the Novel and Other Stories*, p.85.

54.Kurt Vonnegut, *Slaughterhouse-Five* (1969; New York: A Dell Book, 1971), p.172.

55.Gilbert Sorrentino, *Mulligan Stew* (New York: Grove Press, 1979), p.257.

56.Ibid., p.89.

57.Ibid., p.154.

58.Ibid., p.89.

59.Ibid., p.154.

60.Ibid., p.276-77.

61.Philip Roth, *Deception* (New York: Simon and Schuster, 1990), p.190.

62.Federman, Raymond, *The Voice in the Closet* (Madison, Wis.: Coda Press Inc., 1979), p.4.

63.Ibid., p.15.

64.Kurt Vonnegut, *Breakfast of Champions* (New York: Delacorte Press, 1973), p.15.

65.Ibid., p.225.

66.Ibid., p.15.

67.Ibid., p.219.

68.Ibid., p.293.

69.Philip Roth, *The Facts*, pp.164, 184, 166.

70.Philip Roth, *The Counterlife*, pp.226-32.

71.Ibid., pp.304, 316-17.

72.John Irving, *The World According to Garp*, p.162.

73.Ibid., p.162.

74.O'Brien, Tim, *The Things They Carried* (1990; New York, Penguin, 1991), pp.180-181.

75.Philip Roth, *The Counterlife*, p.317.

76.Jerome Klinkowitz, *Literary Disruptions: The Making of a Post-Contemporary American Fiction* (Urbana: University of Illinois Press, 1975), p.198.

77.Brian McHale, *Postmodernist Fiction* (New York and London: Methuen, 1987), p.204.

78.Vladimir Nabokov, *Pale Fire* (1962; New York: Berkley Books, 1968), p.202.

79.Wendy Steiner, "Ending up with two of everything," *Times Literary Supplement*, July 7-13, 1989.

80.Kurt Vonnegut, *Mother Night*, p.ix.

81.John Updike, *Bech: A Book* (1970; Greenwich, Conn.: Fawcett, 1971), p.9.

82.Kurt Vonnegut, *Slaughterhouse-Five*, p.125.

83.Ronald Sukenick, *Up*, p.325.

84.Raymond Federman, *Take It or Leave It*, chap.XIX, no page numbering.

85.Kurt Vonnegut, *Breakfast of Champions*, pp. 2, 193.

86.Joan Didion, *Democracy*, p.16.

87.Quoted in Bryan Cheyette's review of *The Facts*, "Tales of a walking text," *Times Literary Supplement*, February 17-23, 1989.

88.Philip Roth, *Operation Shylock*, p.115.

89.Jerzy Kosinski, *The Hermit of 69th Street* (1988; New York: Zebra, 1991), pp.50, 504-505.

90.Heide Ziegler, *John Barth* (London and N.Y.: Methuen, 1986), p.49.

91.John Barth, *The Friday Book* (New York: Putnam, 1984), p.22.

92.Frederick Karl, *American Fictions: 1940-1980: A Comprehensive History and Critical Evaluation* (New York: Harper and Row, 1983), p.457.

93.John Barth, *LETTERS* (New York: Putnam, 1979), p.84 .

94.Kurt Vonnegut, *Slaughterhouse-Five*, p.206.

95.Philip Roth, *Operation Shylock*, p.73.

96.Norman Mailer, *The Armies of the Night* (New York: New American Library, Signet, 1968), pp.26-27, 54-55.

97.Truman Capote, *Music for Chameleons* (1980; London: Sphere Books, 1981), pp. 144, 233.

98.Ronald Sukenick, *The Death of the Novel and Other Stories*, p.47.

99.William H. Gass, *In the Heart of the Heart of the Country*, pp.xviii, xli.

100.Eugene Goodheart, "Four Decades of Contemporary Fiction," in Boris Ford, ed., *American Literature* (London: Penguin, 1988), p.629, Earl Shorris in "The well-spoken passions of William H. Gass," *Harper's*, May, 1972.

101.Gerald Graff, *Literature Against Itself: Literary Ideas in Modern Society* (Chicago and London: Chicago Univ. Press, 1979), p.180.

102.John Barth, *LETTERS*, p.189.

103.John Barth, *Sabbatical*, p. 112.

104.Ibid., p.190.

105.Philip Roth, *My Life as a Man*, (London: Corgi Books, 1976), p.114.

106.Philip Roth, *Reading Myself and Others* (New York: Farrar, Straus, Giroux, 1975), p.165.

107.Roth, Philip, *A Philip Roth Reader* (London: Penguin, 1984), p.480.

108.Philip Roth, *The Ghost Writer* (1979; New York: Fawcett Crest, 1980), pp.151, 210.

109.John Irving, *The World According to Garp* (New York: Dutton, 1978), p.328.

110.Ibid., p.338.

111.Ibid., pp.119, 176.

112.Truman Capote, *Answered Prayers* (1987; London: Abacus, 1988), p.49.

113.Philip Roth, *The Counterlife*, p.316.

CHAPTER TWO

AMBIVALENT DESIGNS:
THE WRITER-HERO ON EDGE

TO BE A MAN IN THE CITY

The conflict between the desire for achievement, or movement and spatiality, and a fascination with withdrawal, physical and mental, with disguise or deception, has been at work in American fiction after World War II.* Beat writers manifestly exploit the vast space of the American continent (Kerouac) or the energy of the city (Holmes) in an effort to escape society, to go inward, to fantasize. The writers of the next generation, both postmodernists and realists attracted by or converted to metafiction, similarly integrate the need to contain American complexity and vastness with a compulsion to escape, to find meaning beyond the society's social dictates and aesthetic conventions. Their heroes want both to embrace and to hide, to live out the impulse for commitment, exploration and physical adventure, and to assume extreme individualism, eccentricity, and moral aloofness.

Barth's 1982 *Sabbatical* clearly illustrates these polar urges, a need to contain vast spacial experiences combined with a search for the inwardness required of writing. But the vantage point from which recent writer-heroes survey American actuality is typically not a boat, or the road, but the urban milieu, specifically New York City: the site of conflict in itself, the primary force that shapes life and work.

---

*Frederick Karl regards postwar American literature as a blend of distinctive European tendencies with traditional American urges, a meeting of the "European sense of time...with American stress on space; European dread with American escape." He adds: "American pastoral had to accommodate European 'counterfeit'; American openness, European disguise and invisibility." [*American Fictions: 1940-1980*, p.xiii.]

First person narrators often find it disagreeable, or even repulsive. To Burroughs the city is like the innards of a drug addict, a place from which there is no escape. William Gass' *In the Heart of the Heart of the Country* speaks of cities as places "swollen and poisonous with people" in which novelists "break their pens."[1] To Ken Kesey and his Pranksters New York City is "the great cancer capital of the East," the antithesis of freedom.[2] The writer in Vonnegut's *Mother Night* thinks of the many years spent in New York City as hell, "or not Hell, something worse than Hell."[3] The writer-narrator in Sorrentino's *Mulligan Stew* describes American cities as "interchangeable" places of a "featureless" world.[4] Speaking of the deepening "sickness" of the city, John A. Williams' novelist in *!Click Song* sees it not as a symbol of the decline of his race, as Wright or Baldwin characterized urban rot, but as evidence of "a national and world sickness."[5]

A more complex relationship between the writer and the city emerges whenever he goes beyond mere renunciation and, having engaged in urban experience, discovers the admixture of challenge and possibility. The city's crudity and hostility are complemented, typically, by its excitement and energy. Repulsed and drawn to both, the writer tells us that he fears the darker traits of city life, its danger, its squalor, its inhumanity, its loneliness; but, simultaneously, he sees city life as an indispensable source of pleasure and research territory for his creative urges, as well as a necessary initiation into contemporary American experience.

In *Up*, the Sukenick persona stresses the fact that completing his novel cost him "five years of slum life." He describes the run-down tenement house in which he lived, the battles with the increasingly daring rats, the depressing neighborhood.[6] But he also admits that the wretchedness of New York was a necessary experience. Along with the squalor the city gave him, a fledgling writer, literary identity and confidence:

> Well I mean you have to pay for everything....When I look up from my book I want to see a wall with an interesting pattern of cracks and seams. I want to see the scars of experience, not the blank of a cold innocence. A tenement

is alive with the generations that have lived in it....I enjoy the poverty....The fights, muggings and murders are real violence not the psychosis of headlines....This is the only place in the country where I've ever felt at home.[7]

"In New York who needs an atom bomb?" muses Lesser, the novelist in Bernard Malamud's *The Tenants* (1971). The city, seen from his vacant tenement house, is a ruined landscape of gloom and apocalyptic devastation. The buildings nearby are either "marked for disappearance" or deliberately reduced to rubble. Happiness and fulfillment are remote, far removed from the depression of city life. Lesser's desire to escape the caged dullness of New York is expressed in the opening of *The Tenants*:

Lesser catching sight of himself in his lonely glass wakes to finish his book....In the distance mournful blasts of a vessel departing the harbor. Ah, if I could go where it's going.[8]

But he does not want to leave New York, or to move out of the abandoned apartment because he feels that the writing project on which he has been working for almost ten years should be completed where it began. New York is "home" because his book was born in the city, site of the affliction and pain he must endure as an artist. Called "The Promised Land," Lesser's novel is about a writer working on a novel, trying to re-create himself through it.

In Malamud's *Dubin's Lives* (1979) the writer-protagonist suggests that the modern man is pitifully vulnerable when he tries to comprehend life outside the city, that retreat from it is disappointing and potentially dangerous. William Dubin, a writer in his fifties, a former city dweller who once "hungrily sought signs - promises ? - of the natural world on city streets," is now settled on a nine-acre property in upstate New York near the Vermont border. Here he takes long walks, observes the countryside, links his stubborn ambition to finish a book to his relation to nature, hopes it will "teach him - not sure what - perhaps to bring forth the self he sought - defined self, best self?" He has written a biography of Henry David Thoreau, the author who has taught him to rely on the outdoors, its rhythms, its changing seasons, its relevance to life. But Dubin feels that in his case much of that experience proves to be evasive, vicarious, a literary pretension, that he is merely a "visitor to nature." When lost in a snowstorm, he realizes he deceives himself by believing he can be part of the world of nature:

> Am I where I think I am? What a mad thing not to have stayed home with my small stationary miseries. Now I risk my life....I am mad to be here.[9]

Saul Bellow's view of city life is more broadly related to contemporary social, cultural, and economic conditions. *Humboldt's Gift* (1975), recounts two writers' experiences in different American cities at different periods. In New York City Von Humboldt Fleisher, the flamboyant modernist poet who rises to fame in the 1930s, achieves intellectual status and influence, then, having lost both in the 1950s, lives a paranoic existence in the squalor of the Bowery. Citrine, a successful writer, confronts, in the newly affluent Chicago of the 1970s, a new and comic mixture, a Rabelaisian carnival of art, money and crime.

> There were beautiful and moving things in Chicago, but culture was not one of them. What we had was a cultureless city pervaded nevertheless by Mind. Mind without culture was the name of the game, wasn't it? How do you like that! It's accurate. I accepted this condition long ago.[10]

"For Bellow," notes Sanford Pinsker, in an observation that applies equally to a number of Bellow's contemporaries, "to describe the inextricable connections between idea and naturalistic landscape, between the junk of randomness and an itch for transcendental relief, is, in effect, to explore 'the city,' for the very term has become shorthand for that place where competing interests and sheer numbers crunch easily together, where mental designs are expressed in their boldest relief."[11] Citrine reflects at length on how inescapably complicated life in American cities has become. Bewildered by its contradictions and tensions, he recognizes that this "moronic inferno" is instructive to the writer, a key to the postwar complexity.[12] Like another Bellow protagonist, Moses Herzog, Citrine is determined to adjust to urban chaos, to relate it to the state of his own self, to discover "what it means to be a man. In a city. In a century."[13]

Humboldt's Gift explores the perplexing mental topography of the American city in a unique and thorough-going manner. Most other authors of writer-novels vacillate between infatuation with urban life and a total rejection of it. As a case in point, Norbert Blei in *The Second Novel: Becoming a Writer* (1978), abandons his wife and leaves for the City. It has the power to transform him, an anonymous stranger, into a literary celebrity:

> I took the New York Central out of Chicago.
> I was insane romantic in love with train depots,
>> restaurant counters, newspapers, books, cigarettes, rain, October, Neon lights, jazz, desert boots, rain coats, beautiful women, myself-the-writer.
>
> ....
>
> I was Thomas Wolfe, whether the rest of the people on the train realized it or not.

But Blei soon realizes that his attempt to embrace New York is futile:

> I accomplished nothing in New York.
>
> ....
>
> I see now how wrong a writer can be.[14]

Often, the writer-hero is fascinated by the city's pervasive sexual ambience.

Blei fantasizes: "I wanted to live alone in Greenwich Village. I wanted a new woman in my bed every night."[15] For Updike's Bech New York City is the place where one discovers a sense of erotic celebration and vitality. "New York was so *sexy*, in memory: the indoorness of it all, amid circumambient peril....On this island of primitive living copulation occurred as casually as among Polynesians."[16] P.B. Jones, the young novelist in Truman Capote's *Answered Prayers* (1987), sees New York City as an intensely sexual experience, "only an orgasm lasting an hour could surpass the bliss of my first year in New York."[17] Norbert Kosky, Kosinski's persona in *The Hermit of 69th Street*, is enthralled by the many sexual attractions of New York:

> To Kosky, Times Square offers easy enlightenment of sexual videorama mixed with societal video drama. This is his American Place Pigalle, with the native pigs and gals galore, the world of undressing, cross-dressing and overdressing. It is a world of its own, and very much on its own.[18]

Like other writers in American fiction, Kosky is more interested in exploiting the thrills of the city, or imitating them, than in trying to comprehend its haunting allure and mixed metaphors.* Alfred Kazin, an astute observer of the synergy between the city and the writer, stresses the latter's growing fascination with the surface allure and excitement of places like New York. Kazin points out the affinity of the city's outward excitement with the current artist's manipulation of reality.

"The 'glitzy' city, with its concomitant violence, is a...godsend to the expert

---

*The term "mixed metaphor" is used in the above quoted scene in the first edition of *The Hermit*. Since I find the later, shortened and altered version of this observation less compelling, I quote the original lines:
> To [Kosky]...Times Square offers easy enlightenment of American burlesque, fused with the challenge of French vaudeville; this is a sexual videorama mixed with spiritual video drama. This is his American Place Pigalle, with the native pigs and gals galore, the world of undressing, cross-dressing and overdressing. It is a world of its own, and very much on its own, a mixed metaphor. [Jerzy Kosinski, *The Hermit of 69th Street* (New York: Seaver Books, 1988), p. 251.]

manipulators of illusion, layout, and news flash. Never were there...so much conspicuous and driveling fantasy manufactured and sold in the name of postmodernist sensationalism, so much music and entertainment in the unsleeping city twenty-four hours a day, so much empty emulation of fashion in the name of creativity."[19]

The attempt to exploit urban delights usually ends in disappointment and grotesque confrontations. Random sexual encounters never result in love, while efforts to preserve the sense of the city's sexual exhilaration miscarry painfully. Capote offers a metaphorical example. His novelist-hero, who tried to safeguard his happy life in New York through marriage, explains why he failed: "Perhaps what I wanted in the way of a wife was the city itself, my happiness there, my sense of the inevitable fame, fortune. Alas, what I married was a girl."[20]

The narrator of Paul Theroux's "Lady Max" (1992), an American novelist who lives in London, similarly confuses the excitements of the big city and women. When he meets a mysterious and sexually attractive London socialite, Lady Max, he sees her as the essence of the seductive exoticism of the city. With time, however, she proves to be an exceedingly brash and egotistical caricature of the "desirable woman" who selfishly manipulates his and others' lives, an ugly, greedy, witch-like figure: "Like London itself - Dickensian in one street, dreary in another, renovated, crass, cozy, dangerous - not one city, but many."[21]

The citified writer in the post-1960s novel is, nearly without exception, a lonely womanizer or sexual adventurer suspended between a perpetual search for the excitement of available women, and a fear of commitment and responsibility. It is here, in the American author's fictional mirror of himself, that claims about the American male being pathologically incapable to deal with love and marriage, or that he is a perennial adolescent characterized by chronic "psychic immaturity," as critics like Leslie Fiedler and Kenneth Lynn observe, are supported by additional, fascinating research material.[22]

The literary artist after World War II lives in a state of permanent conflict with women. Indeed, emotional survival, the success of his work, depend on his ability to confront women, to circumvent marriage, if possible - that is, to make women both available and disposable. To accomplish this, he sometimes renounces the macho role and presents himself as a fragile and troubled case. In her discussion of Vonnegut, Josephine Hendin, observes that "Vonnegut is a culture hero because he *celebrates* male vulnerability....His recognition is that what most men achieve is not satisfaction - the loving wife, the status job, the son to be proud of - but resignation and perseverance in a numbing and draining condition. And for these he breaks out in praise."[23] In Roth's *The Anatomy Lesson* (1983) Zuckerman decides to marry only to protect himself against "the tremendous distraction of women." "He'd married so as never to waste himself on another affair, or go crazy with boredom at another party."[24] Under such flawed conditions, the marriage shortly crumbles, and the distracted novelist-hero looks for sexual satisfaction, however temporary, in fortuitous encounters.

The conflict between the writer and women, handled obliquely in 19th century American fiction, nervously signalled in the first half of this century, becomes increasingly foregrounded after World War II. Beat writers, rekindling the myth of going West, stress companionship with male friends - as opposed to meaningful relationships with women. At the beginning of *On the Road*, Sal Paradise declares that the misery of a failed marriage was replaced by the adventure of male bonding:

> I first met Dean not long after my wife and I split up. I had just gotten over a serious illness that I won't bother to talk about, except that it had something to do with the miserable weary split-up and my feeling that everything was dead. With the coming of Dean Moriarty began the part of my life you could call my life on the road....[25]

Burroughs sees women as the primary repository of an alien virus used by outer space powers to defeat men, who are an utterly useless species, a mistake of creation.

Norman Mailer's hipster heroes treat women as providers of "orgasm therapy," or as adversaries in copulation warfare, not as partners, intellectual or social, in the mental-cultural revolution. Other writers to emerge out of the Beat and Hip ethos similarly see women either as a threat to freedom, or as convenient sexual toys. Henry Miller, whose novels of the 1930s were banned in the States for thirty years, remains the prophet of artistic anger grounded in macho eroticism.

The sixties writer, attuned to fiction's innovative verbal and formal possibilities, discovers that sex and women may be used as convenient referents for the act of writing itself. William Gass writes in the preface to *In the Heart of the Heart of the Country* (1968) that sex is a distinct analogue of fiction because "Writing and reading, like male and female, pain and pleasure, are close but divergent."[26] In Gass' *Willie Master's Lonesome Wife* we are told that "the true kiss comprises a secret exchange of words, for the mouth was made by God to give form and sound to syllables...any intercourse of lips...should be further and more completely understood to be a sweet conclave of heads."[27] For the writer in Norbert Blei's *The Second Novel* the female body is the physical extension of a text: "I once had a woman who would lie down on my pages, and I would turn her over gently to discover the wonders to be read into her body."[28] Kosinski expands the idea into a metaphor to which he devotes several hundred pages of narrative in *The Hermit of 69th Street*. Kosky engages in a prolonged and relentless neurotic-euphoric fixation with the number 69 (highlighted by the title), also 96, turning it (like Pynchon's analogy between the rocket and the phallus), into a central, compulsively articulated emblem of his innumerable porno fantasies and sexual encounters, a hallmark of both his psyche and textual extravagance. In chapter 69, which follows chapter 40, puzzled by the fact that his recent book does not sell, he wonders whether there was not enough of 69 in it.*

---

*Kosky's sexual-literary passions have their current nemesis. His diary (supposedly annotated by "Kosinski" after Kosky's death at sea), is filled with recurring fear that chance sexual encounters mean contracting AIDS. A dilemma related to this concern, Kosky muses, is whether a literary character can be infected by his author.

Barth treats the proximity of writing and sex in a consistent and compulsive manner. Musing about the mysteries of the funhouse, Ambrose, the budding literary artist in *Lost in the Funhouse,* comes to realize that sex is "the whole point" of being in the labyrinths of life or fiction. On his part, Barth explains, on the dust jacket of the book, that "technique in art...has about the same value as technique in love making."[29] In *Chimera* (1972), a Barth-like Genie tells Scheherazade that "the very relation between teller and told was by nature erotic," that "writing and reading, or telling and listening, were literally ways of making love," that elements of fiction such as exposition, climax and denouement are reflected in "the rhythm of sexual intercourse from foreplay through coitus to orgasm and release."[30] In *Sabbatical,* which is subtitled "A Romance," telling stories and making love are likened to twins, another Barth motif. Looking back at his literary and nautical adventure, shared with him by his sexy and loving wife, the writer-narrator says: "The doing and the telling, our writing and our loving - they're twins. That's our story."[31] Emphasizing the natural "coupling" proclivity of writing and loving, one of the protagonists of *The Tidewater Tales* speaks of "swapping stories" and "swapping kisses," of "Sex and stories, stories and sex. Teller and listener changing positions and coming together till they're unanimous."[32]

If such amiable parables of women as obliging recipients of men's sexual urges become a conspicuous design of the new fiction about writers, they do not create the dominant tone. More typically, male protagonists describe a state of war with their wives or lovers, presenting themselves as victims of female betrayal, viciousness, or fanaticism.* The novelist in James Purdy's *Cabot Wright Begins* deals with a wife who cynically manipulates his literary career, who makes him feel lonely, desperate and artistically insecure. The two young writers in Philip Roth's *My Life as a Man* discover that the women they marry, partly to confront their Jewish

---

*Frederick Karl sees Heller, Mailer, and Bellow in this respect as "war novelists" who have moved from the violence of war to the violence of marriage. Philip Roth, who did not write a war novel, describes domestic situations, Karl argues, as a "combat scene." [*American Fictions: 1940-1980,* p.497.]

background, partly out of their youthful, literature-oriented idealism, are unpredictable and crazed to the point of being unreal. Maureen, Tarnopol's wife, is a compulsive liar and a vampire-like psychopath (who does bite),* who provides him not with the "intractability" needed for the "complicated fictions of moral anguish," but with "the intractability of soap opera."[33] Bellow's Citrine is dragged to court by his ex-wife and her lawyers who, on the assumption that he has "a proven ability to earn big sums" as a bestselling author, demand alimony, settlements and bonds which nearly ruin him financially. Moreover, Citrine's mistress wants him for his name and his money while she sleeps with, and later marries, a rich undertaker, leaving her son in the writer's care. Successful as a writer, Citrine experiences failure as lover and husband. He thinks that marriage in America has become a state of war: "Real Americans are supposed to suffer with their wives, and wives with husbands." Yet men's chances are not, he explains to his lawyer, as good as women's: "If I meet her demands she makes brand-new ones. Since the Emancipation Proclamation there's been a secret struggle in this country to restore slavery by other means."[34]

The hero's vulnerability is more acute, his nervousness more pronounced, when he deals with women who manifest a need to be emancipated, or who are artistically and/or professionally successful. In Holmes' *Go* (1952), Paul Hobbes, the writer, regards Liza Adler as "an alarming experience," an aggressor, a threat. "A violent Marxist with a quick, destructive tongue and a mental agility that was new to Hobbes in women," she battles with him and his ideas, mocks him "to his face," and (paradigmatically in the genre) stages a nervous breakdown before she goes out of his life.[35] In Mailer's "The Man Who Studied Yoga," Sam Slovoda "feels uneasy" with his wife, Eleanor, a painter and an interior decorator, who is also a competent observer of her husband's mental clutter, because she can deal with confusion

---

*In *The Facts*, the Roth persona tells us that his own lover and wife, Josie (Josephine Jensen), "a little gem of treacherous invention," was a prototype of Maureen in *My Life as a Man*. She engineered a pregnancy test fraud which "parallels almost exactly" Maureen's trick. Zuckerman, with whom Roth corresponds in the book, typically negates this claim. He points out that Roth is unfair to the woman because he deprives her of her own point of view and turns her into "a bloodsucking monster" with "fangs!" [*The Facts*, pp.175, 107.]

without neurotic symptoms or reliance on analysis. She is "competing with him" and she "does not often give Sam what he needs most, a steady flow of uncritical encouragement to counteract the harshness with which he views himself."[36] In Hemingway's *The Garden of Eden* the novelist's wife tries to debauch him, then to destroy him as an artist, by using her liberated sexuality, daring and money. The "devil things" she wants to practice on her honeymoon include the swapping of sexual roles, a lesbian affair with an attractive stranger, and her husband's commitment to sleep with each woman in turn.[37] These 1950s signals of writers' nervousness about the emergence of emancipated women are increasingly pronounced in the later decades. The fictions of Mailer, Updike, Irving and Kosinski frequently focus on the ongoing struggle between emasculated males and self-confident and sexually assertive women. Kosinski's Kosky (*The Hermit of 69th Street*) confesses that his fear of such women is greater than his creative anxieties:

Writes Kosky on the margin: I am a writer; a wordsmith who works with words, and who loves playing with them, as much as playing with women. But while creative women still threaten me as much as, say, the noncreative threatened August Strindberg, words do not.[38]

In Paul Theroux's "Lady Max," the novelist-hero is afraid that the rich and brilliant woman he adores is a witch that makes him "feel like an idiot," in fact wants to "suck my soul out of my body." "Part of her witchery came from her power to spread confusion, and the rest of her witchery was her beauty. But I was still confused."[39] In Theroux's massive *My Secret History* such fears are more closely examined. Andre Parent points to the novelist's rejection of stable and trusting relations with his female partners. He fears women because they epitomize settled life, something he desires yet cannot tolerate. When he marries Jenny, an English woman, he seems content; she has set him free to write and to travel. Though he soon has a house and son and his career as a writer is launched, he is unsatisfied - what he misses is a life that is "a system of secrets."

I saw that I had lived my whole life that way, drawing energy from secrecy, and feeding my imagination on what I kept hidden.[40]

Parent finds it easy to create for himself two different lives, "the intensity of two of everything," including two women in two different countries. Though living "in the cracks between them," in an adaptable expandable space that belongs to neither, brings loneliness, he feels deeply that he is really alive, protecting a literary sensibility.

I was living two lives, and I knew I was a slightly different person with each woman - lied to each of them, or chose a different version of the truth for them....They invented me; I invented them....Wasn't I a new man when I was alone?

Deprived of this secrecy and loneliness, he is unhappy. "Was that everyone's condition - that we were each of us unknown?," Parent muses, "I did not talk. I listened. I watched. And in my silence I became invisible."[41]

Andre Parent follows the self-justified macho tradition so emphatically written into American fiction by writers like Ernest Hemingway, Henry Miller, or Norman Mailer, the tradition of constructing crude pseudo-philosophical defenses against women, of treating them coldly, with a sense of detachment and reduced emotions, of seeing them as useful sex objects, or sycophantic admirers, but never as companions in creativity. It is also the tradition of a fear that marriage is a threat to the artist. Hemingway's writers, Robert Cohn in *The Sun Also Rises*, Harry in "The Snows of Kilimanjaro," Robert Davies in *Islands in the Stream*, or David Bourne in *The Garden of Eden*, maintain that women, when they become wives, destroy or jeopardize writing. To be a successful writer, writer-heroes recurringly declare, one has to avoid marriage for as long as possible.[*] Roth's Zuckerman announces in all seriousness that being attached to a wife is an impediment for a writer, especially when he becomes rich and famous, "a sex symbol to the hordes," that he himself does not "have the aptitude for a binding, sentimental attachment to one woman for life....Maybe my aptitude is for changing partners...." He prefers "one lovely new woman every five years."[42]

Indeed, in the postwar novel the woman is no longer seen as muse. Bernard Malamud's *Dubin's Lives* (1979) is an apparent exception.[**] The fifty-six-year-old William Dubin regards the twenty-two-year-old Fanny Bick as a last chance to taste the kinds of passions he is writing about in his own book. "One writes lives he can't live," he muses. A successful biographer, now working on the life of D.H. Lawrence, he knows that biographies, "ultimately fiction," are maps of human life and fonts of spiritual energy.[43] Lawrence is for him a tantalizing paragon who teaches how to feed on women's vitality and youth. Yet the affair with a young woman becomes a lasting distraction for Dubin, not a source of inspiration. On a trip to Venice she deceives him. Mortified by the fact that his muse is unfaithful, Dubin returns to his wife, a neurotic woman with whom he is sexually impotent. More than two years of solitude follow filling Dubin's life with much reflective pain and persistent longings for Fanny. The British novelist haunts him: "Lawrence would have scorned him for the little he'd had yet lived on."[44] When Fanny reappears offering more mature attitudes and love, Dubin feels he is again a gifted man, a superb biographer. They meet on the nearby farm she has purchased, become lovers, wrestle in bed, "she with her youth; he with his wiles."[45]

Although Malamud's tale seems anomalous among the writer-novels of the last few decades, it ultimately reveals the same refusal to treat women as the source of artistic vitality or inspiration. Despite living out his other life, Dubin remains

---

[*]This attitude proves purely "fictional" in view of novelists' real lives. Almost all authors discussed so far marry, some of them several times, and continue to produce books.

[**]Malamud said that the novel was a reflection on what his own experience "totaled up to." [In Ralph Tyler's "A Talk With the Novelist," *The New York Times Book Review*, Feb.18, 1979.]

dissatisfied. One day he tells Fanny that he is "a family man," has work to do, that "there are other things" in his life.[46] Dozens of other postwar men-of-letters as heroes similarly flee or resist their female partners. Happy marriages or stable attachments with women nearly disappear from their lives. They are replaced by random love affairs, various brief sexual rituals, porno spectacles, multiple lovers, sometimes assaults on women, even killings. Sexual anger and latent vengeance are often displayed and made functional, the source of the writer's strength and identity.

In Philip Roth's *The Anatomy Lesson*, the novelist, tormented by an undiagnosed disease, malicious critics, and a writing block finds comfort in four mistresses who visit his apartment in turns. He needs these women for therapy and companionship, but treats each with notable nonchalance. When he realizes they are unable to help him refurbish his life, he decides to "be rid of" them all.[47] The writer in Federman's *The Twofold Vibration* is evicted from an expensive hotel for chasing, nakedly, a girl (also naked) in the lobby, then carrying her on his shoulder to his room where he, "mad...ferocious in his sexual excitement," ravishes her in front of two other naked women.[48] In Sukenick's *Up*, a woman is offered to the writer by a friend who says that "She'll do anything....She's had three abortions." The narrator says she should be proud to be used by men: "You're the sexual revolution. On the hoof."[49] A Sukenick-like character in *Out* lets a woman fellate him, then punches her in the face and pushes her against the wall, reminding his bloodied and surprised victim "you forgot to say thank you."[50] The various male characters in Kosinski's novels seek women out for brief, passionate relationships in which they are often treated brutally, or, at best, as porno-fantasy objects to be enjoyed and discarded. When a woman says to Kosky, in *The Hermit of 69th Street*: "Sex with you is like reading Milton....It's nonpoetic. No foreplay. No rhyme," the novelist responds: "I'm prosaic, not poetic. Besides, rhyme restricts. Sex is a free outpetaling - not outpedaling of the lotus."[51] In *Blind Date* (1977), Levanter remembers how he, at the age of fifteen, rapes a woman in a "blind date" manner. Held and assaulted from behind, she cannot identify her assailant.

For Tim Madden, a former boxer and a part-time writer, in *Tough Guys Don't*

Dance (1984), violence is a manly, purifying, self-preserving force. He wakes up one morning to discover a tattoo on his arm and blood on the seat of his Porsche; later he finds a severed female head in his secret marijuana patch. He must find out whether he is the actual killer or the framed victim. Madden immediately suspects a link between his predicament and the fact that his wife has recently abandoned him, for he has never fully understood why she, a rich woman, decided to marry him. To expose "the abyss beneath my vanity?" To do "the devil's work?"[52] Was she the witch she said she wanted to be? Nightmares and panic envelop Madden as he tries to answer these questions. Like Mailer's other existential heroes, he attempts to untangle the mysteries of his tortured psyche by asserting himself as a violent conqueror of women - the agents of the corruptive or malevolent forces around him.

The way Tony Lamont, the failing and increasingly paranoid writer-figure in Sorrentino's *Mulligan Stew*, denounces a fellow-novelist for a gratuitous use of sex in story-telling might apply to the material of Mailer's *Tough Guys*:

> The idea of a novel about a writer writing a novel is truly *old hat*. Nothing further can be done with the genre, a genre that was exhausted at its moment of conception. Nobody cares about that idea any more, and Dermot knew it. To rescue his shambles of a book he added scenes of gratuitous sexuality, so crassly done as to cause all but the most debased reader to throw the book down in dismay and disgust....It is hardly a book at all but a grim exercise in the soiled terrain of the marketplace, a playing to the grandstand for the transitory rewards of quick money and notoriety, neither of which the author received in the quantities desired.[53]

But Lamont is disingenuous since he exploits, as a writer, the same material. Indeed, his own "novel" is filled with steamy sex scenes linked to well-known literary icons, including Daisy Buchanan who, as ever tired with Tom, "debase[s] herself" in a brothel for the pleasure of ogling men, a pornographic scene Fitzgerald could not have included in *The Great Gatsby*.[54] Lamont becomes a parody of himself, while Sorrentino reflects on the current abuse of sexuality as a literary theme.

Some female characters of the novels discussed here, though their judgments are filtered through the prevailing male point of view and subject to the language of male authors, occasionally protest men's abuse and exploitation of women. Maria, Zuckerman's lover and wife to be, in Roth's *The Counterlife*, is angry that the novelist manipulates her life, reducing her to a "a series of fictive propositions." "You want to play reality-shift? Get yourself another girl. I'm leaving," she says...and does disappear from the novel.[55] She "reappears" in *The Facts* and points out to Zuckerman, now her husband: "I sometimes think that men have a root neurosis about women....It's really a sort of suspicion....men are a bit afraid of women....that's why they behave as they do."[56] Later, in *Deception*, the hero's lover is annoyed by the fact that she is a part of his notebook of the novel in which women are both recognizable persons and appear in fictive situations. Confused, unable to tell story-telling from seduction, she says:

> You don't know how to leave *anything* alone. Just to give voice to the woman is never enough for you. You will not just drown in her cuntliness. You must always submerge her and distort her in your hero's stupid, artificial *plot.*[57]

American female authors, on the other hand, rarely present themselves in fiction as writers. Whole areas of women's experience as novelists are virtually untouched in the postwar novel. Erica Jong is a notable exception. Like no other female author in the States she is eager to tell what it means to be the female counterpart in the sex wars of the literary profession. Her alter ego, the celebrated and guilt-ridden novelist Isadora Wing, knows well, in *How to Save Your Own Life* (1977), that she should be "grateful and obligated" to enjoy her status as a firmly established writer and have normal family life, above all a husband "who'd put up with my success."

> After all, he hadn't left me when my novel *Candida Confesses* (which everyone but me seemed to think was so outrageous) became a best seller. And he hadn't left me when all his patients asked whether he was a character in the book. And he hadn't left me when I did the unpardonable thing of becoming a public figure....[58]

Isadora rejoices in being female and successful, in having a man's freedom to bring sex into life and art, in acting out alluring "itches" which she knew were "un-American."[59] She knows how to use men, or defy them when thwarted. She has the rhetorical skills and the determination to act as if she were declaring a sexual-artistic revolution for her gender, as if she were the angry-elated female version of Henry Miller.[*]

Yet, Isadora reveals a sense of chronic vulnerability and guilt. Her dependence on men and faith in traditional values lead to intermittent urges to abandon art, to return to conventional female roles. She sees her life as a string of disappointments and indicates that a female writer is always suspended between a need to subordinate herself and to hurdle society's barriers, between wanting to be uniquely feminine and having to live out a male concept of the artist, a role that, she is intelligent enough to realize, no longer exists.[**] She is torn by forces that are the

---

[*]In her recent *The Devil at Large: Erica Jong on Henry Miller* (1993), Jong actually draws, with typical fierceness and audacity, an analogy between the lives, careers, reputations, and overall artistic and moral relevance of herself and Henry Miller, who praised her *Fear of Flying* noting the parallels to his *Tropic of Cancer*. She claims that Miller's fate in the hands of American readers, prudish, torn between sexophobia and sexomania, has become her own.

[**]In her *A Portrait of the Artist as a Young Woman: The Writer as Heroine in American Literature* (1983), Linda Huf, while comparing the image of the male artist-hero with characters created by female writers, points out that women often not only do not resemble the male models of artistic behavior, as Maurice Beebe maintained in his *Ivory Towers and Sacred Founts*, but often invert them. Whereas male artists use women as muse, Huf observes, female heroines do not have a need for male ones, in fact, have no muses at all. Men as writers tend to be shy and passive, have feminine traits, while female artists possess "masculine" traits. Huf's assertions, somewhat contrived and bogus, are further impaired by the limitation she herself tries to correct. She analyzes female artist-characters by referring to the male heroes as outlined in Beebe's book, a work whose assumptions do not apply to the novels of the second half of the twentieth century.

female equivalent of what the male writer went through a century earlier.

AGAINST IT, I WRITE, AND WRITE WHAT?

The American writer has long been signalling, in personal notes and in fictional versions of his own life, that furtive, immobilizing forces of the community, the administrative system, or political attitudes intrude when he embarks on serious work, that he ends up isolated, exposed to frustration and artistic paralysis. In the "Custom-House" Hawthorne recalls that while a state employee he was being overtaken by a "wretched numbness," a kind of intellectual "torpor," which threatened (but actually stimulated) his artistic growth.[60] Melville's frustration over his loss of popular and critical acclaim after the publication of *Moby Dick* translated itself into a withdrawal from public life and a bitterly pessimistic vision of a writer in *Pierre*. But such discontent, patiently communicated within a literary means that was ultimately complicit with the culture it attempted to expose, is insignificant, merely a ripple, when compared with the mental estrangement and rage that occur in American fictions about writers - especially those of the 1970s and the 1980s. The disrespect for the social and cultural values of America is strikingly radical, the vilification obsessive, the anger direct and personal. In Sorrentino's *Splendide-Hôtel* (1973), for example, the first person narrator thus speaks of the writer's inevitable descent into impotence and idiocy in confrontation with American reality:

...we all stand now as idiots in the face of the mass devastation of feeling that abounds....Well, so the country is dying and against its death I can do - nothing. What little I have to offer, all find useless. A government of scoundrels, a people numb with hatred and fear. Against it, I write, and write what? B? Betty Boop. Boop-boop-a-doop. Babel. Babble. The false poet has written a false novel, the language further corrupted. This rubbish will sour and destroy the soil. I write B. What will put an end to our delighted suicide?[61]

The novels of the last few decades are full of such harangues. Typically, the writer-character is the outraged spokesman, the irate and confused victim of an immense disorder. Henry Bech, in Updike's *Bech: A Book*, links his artistic numbness with America's corrupt power over him. "No revolutionary has concerned himself with our oppression," he complains, "with the silken mechanism whereby America reduces her writers to imbecility and cozenage."[62]

Likewise, Peter Tarnopol, the writer-protagonist in Philip Roth's *My Life as a Man*, speaks of being confronted with a reality as "obdurate and recalcitrant and in addition as awful as any I could have wished for in my bookish dreams."[63] It vexes him profoundly, drains him of energy. Also, Susan Turner, one of the two author-protagonists in Barth's *Sabbatical*, declares that her rage with America gives her "a craving to spit on several US ex-Presidents dead and alive, their secretaries of state, joint chiefs of staff, and CIA directors."[64] Finally, Bruce Gold, in Joseph Heller's *Good as Gold* (1979), believes his country has reached the ultimate in chaos, a terminal condition. He claims there is "no longer anything legal to be done under the American system of government to discourage crime, decrease poverty, improve the economy, or nullify the influences of neglect." He hopes to write a book entitled "Every Change Is For The Worse," in which he will report on how "the most advanced and penultimate stage of a civilization was attained when chaos masqueraded as order."[65]

These outbursts of uncontrolled anger reveal a deep-rooted resentment not only of what America has become but also of the author's own sense of complicity. Behind both lurks a desire for a change, a renewal, a securing of an unadulterated life. "I'm as full of shit as Lyndon Johnson....I'm nothing but his little old alter ego," declaims Norman Mailer, in *The Armies of the Night*, on stage in a Washington theatre before the peace march.[66] He deliberately disgraces himself in front of the audience he is supposed to charge with political awareness so as to demonstrate, with astounding intellectual mastery, that he is part of America's degeneracy, of her being internally divided, violent, possibly insane, headed for self-destruction.

Kurt Vonnegut's persona in *Breakfast of Champions* declares that American society is uncommonly acquisitive, violent, racist, hypocritical, indifferent to arts and obsessed with quantifiable data. It has always been that way. The people who settled the country were "pirates" disposed to "cheat and rob and kill" the indigenous people. Today, though "by far the richest and most powerful country on the planet," America spreads immorality everywhere and intimidates other countries by "threatening to shoot big rockets at them or to drop things on them from airplanes." He, as hero, for whom *Breakfast* is a "fiftieth birthday present," admits he is "programmed to perform childishly - to insult 'The Star-Spangled Banner,' to scrawl pictures of a Nazi flag and an asshole and a lot of other things with a felt-tipped pen." A crude picture "of an asshole" follows, an awkward gesture of artistic defiance, but also of self-purification. He wants to empty himself radically of his culture's worn-out values so as to replenish it with new ones: "I have no culture, no harmony in my brains. I can't live without a culture any more."[67] Meanwhile, he demonstrates cruelty to characters who would like to make their lives sympathetic, or useful. So does Trout, his creation. Disenchanted with the American system he is eager to poison the minds of his readers.

Yet, self-renewal, individual or national, may not be feasible, the Vonnegut persona intimates throughout the novel. The atrocities of our civilization impact the writer with a devastating force, become a nearly physical intrusion, an unavoidable conflict. In *Slaughterhouse-Five*, the hero thus complains of being beset by ongoing political horrors:

Robert Kennedy, whose summer home is eight miles from the home I live in all year round, was shot two nights ago. He died last night. So it goes.

Martin Luther King was shot a month ago. He died too. So it goes.

And every day my Government gives me a count of corpses created by military science in Vietnam. So it goes.

Like Mailer in *The Armies*, the Vonnegut persona sees the country's present-day depravity as a continuation of a complex and deep-rooted tradition of arrogance and violence, a tradition he rejects:

> My Father died many years ago now - of natural causes. So it goes. He was a sweet man. He was a gun nut, too. He left me his guns. They rust.[68]

Charlie Citrine in Bellow's *Humboldt's Gift* feels abused, blocked in his work, brought to the brink of a psychological crisis by the condition of contemporary American life, to him a new brand of barbarism. He sees his society as a rigged system that "trains you in distraction" because it is deformed by materialism, sexual freedom, perversity and violence.[69] "History," muses Charlie, "had created something new in the USA, namely crookedness with self-respect or duplicity with honor." It has also filled the country with a dangerous malady - boredom, a peculiar lack of "personal connection with the external world," or what may be called "hyperactive...restlessness," a spiritual numbness, the mind's sloth. People infected by it "just sleep, and eat and play and fuss and sleep again."[70] Charlie believes that he himself has been the victim of this affliction. Then he hastens to explain he has managed to free himself of it:

> As I was lying stretched out in America, determined to resist its material interests and hoping for redemption by art, I fell into a deep snooze that lasted for years and decades. Evidently I didn't have what it took....But there's no excuse, really. Luckily, I'm still alive and perhaps there's even some time still left.[71]

In John Irving's *The World According to Garp*, the title character sees his society as being plagued by a mixture of violence and craziness, a monstrous force -

remembering his son's mispronunciation of "undertow," Garp calls it the Under Toad - which destroys routinely and invidiously. People around him die, are violated or maimed in gory and bizarre ways - or they involve themselves (by sexual or political fanaticism) in situations that turn into horror. His mother, the author of a celebrated feminist autobiography, is shot at a political rally. Garp himself will die violently. His death, his publisher thinks, "in its random, stupid, and unnecessary qualities - comic and ugly and bizarre - underlined everything Garp had ever written about how the world works."[72] Before this occurs, however, Garp's life is a valiant, sometimes obsessive and comical struggle with various expressions of violence.

These visions of America, vivid and sharply etched, are often even more intensely vitriolic in works of metafiction, where America is shown as a system absurdly distorted and brutalized, stupefying and infuriating, a land despoiled by mechanization and violence, filled with countless dangers and neuroses, even as a gigantic garbage site or as a storehouse of wickedness.* Beset by such a pernicious system which has only lately gone wrong, the hero laments, in language that is frequently indignant, aggressive and scatological, that he is unable to function as writers once did. He complains that the insanities of America drain him, fill him with abhorrence, violate his privacy, distract his work, that his attempts to fight back and to protect himself fail - or lead to spectacles of mortification.

Yet this bitter criticism, to some extent the result of the post 1960s ethos of unprecedented, perhaps, but not absolute freedom of expression, is only vaguely grounded in the complex socio-political phenomena that are ultimately to blame. Solutions are rarely suggested, ideologies remain irrelevant. The approach is anecdotal rather than analytical, individual rather than representational, emotional rather than objective. Expressed frequently in a neurotic or exhibitionistic manner, defiance is finally a pose, a consciously flaunted and perversely audacious gesture of disobedience and anger. Judith Horne, a writer in one of Joyce Carol Oates'

---

*Images of America as a garbage site are dominant in Richard Brautigan's *Trout Fishing in America* and *In Watermelon Sugar*.

stories, thus defines the easy rebelliousness of the American artists and intellectuals today: "Their defiance of their government might be published in foot-high headlines, or engraved in stone, and they will never be arrested or executed or even interrogated. So they appear formidable in their brazenness, their eerie invulnerability, like mythic creatures, demi-gods, or golems not quite possessed of souls."[73]

Though he shows himself as the victim of America's disorder, the writer-figure often speaks and acts in ways that reveal a remarkable capability, usually acquired in the course of the tale, to survive and adjust to the dislocations and atrocities he describes, to be "in dialogue" with them.* More importantly, he has a need to emulate them in art or use them as a mode of creative renewal. No longer paralyzed by the postwar horrors to the point of paranoia and artistic deadlock (as in the 1950s), fiction's man-of-letters in the 1970s and 1980s becomes a hypnotized observer and eager absorber of what he deplores. His profession's own intricacies, derangements, or insanities are now less important to him.** What comes to the forefront of his attention is the outer evidences of native corruption, the moral dissipation, the violence, the underworld. Gone, even openly repudiated, are some of the older patterns of artistic responsibility and propriety we find in novels about artists from Hawthorne to Hemingway. The writer of Capote's *Answered Prayers*, though ultimately himself a loser, recounts with pride his ability to combine literary ambition with other roles, i.e. being bisexual, working as a masseur or a body-guard: "at last I wasn't a deadbeat expatriate, an aimless loser; I was a man with a mission in life, an *assignment*...tomorrow I would buy a .38 revolver and start practice at a shooting range."[74]

Many heroes declare that fascination with America's psychosis and corruption is ultimately creative. Vonnegut's outlandish self-reflection in *Breakfast*

---

*Irving's Garp is an exception here, but violence kills him as a man, not as an artist.

**Nabokov with his *Pale Fire* (1962) and *Look at the Harlequins!* (1974) is, characteristically, different in this respect.

of Champions is as much an immersion in revulsion as it is a search for meaning and innocence, a need to review one's own biographical past, to destroy the kind of artist one had been, to regenerate one's fiction at the time of a midlife crisis. When he tells Trout "I am cleansing and renewing myself for the very different sorts of years to come," he expresses a desire to reconcile himself to the reality he had not expected to experience.[75] He also hopes to challenge something larger, to question the outdated poses and pretensions of the American writer in general, to expose the artificiality of the whole literary culture in America.

In *The Armies of the Night* the Mailer persona defends his bizarre public exhibitions and confrontations. He claims that the events of the march transformed him as a writer, made him innovative, self-aware, existentially attuned to his times and his own untamed and quixotic self. He is also convinced that his drunken, clownish showmanship awakens and animates the audience of the pre-march rally at a Washington theatre, that he possesses the power to make Americans courageous and motivated again. The country's problems may yet be solved, he tells us; America may again become "a new world brave and tender, artful and wild."[76] His being, as he formulates it earlier in *Advertisements for Myself*, "destructive and therefore useful," assumes the tone of Whitmanesque idealism, bardic confidence and aesthetic determination.[77]

Other lamentations about America's viciousness contain similar, variously and imaginatively realized testimonies of the eagerness to examine the country's new social-cultural disruptions, to embrace them, to incorporate them in art. Writers eagerly explore transgressions and perversions, the liberated sexuality, the new extravagance. They experience, highlight, and contain them in new and bold uses of language. Bellow's Citrine is determined to study, humbly and honestly, the country's transmutations and confusions, to learn to live with the obscenities and depravities of Chicago - a new and permanent phase of American civilization. He hopes he can find more sober and more sensible ways of dealing with America than his predecessor, Humboldt. He also wants to overcome America's callousness and perfidy towards writers. When the publishers of his book "Some Americans," subtitled "The Sense of Being in the United States," want him to abandon the project offering to forgive the twenty-thousand advance, he not only refuses to do so, but starts "perversely" writing part II because, he tells himself, "My life was in great disorder."[78]

Irving's Garp is disgusted by the prevalence of violence and insanity in contemporary America, yet he is endlessly mystified by the mechanics of its urgency and proliferation in the society. When he sees his own fiction deteriorate and his writing temporarily blocked, he realizes that he is unable to imagine situations that would match life's gruesomeness. The book he later writes, "The World According to Bensenhaver," a story of rape and carnage purporting to be true and actual, which Garp's publisher calls "an X-rated soap opera," brings him massive popularity and money, though the publication finally leads to his violent death.[79]

While focusing on violence in all its aspects, the hero himself seldom resorts to physical aggression, or sees himself as an agent of corruption.[*] The fiendish ironies and brutal fantasies he commonly exploits do not violate the barriers between his literary imagination, and his life. Even Norman Mailer, who recognizes and continues to probe violence as a key to creative change and personal improvement, does not turn writers into users of redundant criminality or cruelty. Stephen Rojack, who in *An American Dream*, finds new and fuller realizations of the self through rape, murder and other forms of violence, is not cast as a functional artist or writer. Neither is Tim Madden, in *Tough Guys Don't Dance*, a foul-mouthed psychopath who takes drugs, drinks hard and acts violently. Though he calls himself a writer (with a mind reduced to "a book where pages are missing"), he hardly ever mentions his professional side (except when he praises Updike's talent to describe pubic hair) and admits he is "not good enough writer to say what I really feel."[80] The dread which envelops him can hardly be seen as a transmutation of a writer's terror. Or a

---

[*]As does, for instance, the British critic, Duncan Williams. Williams believes that writers help "saturate" life with violence and animalism and are "to a remarkable degree responsible" for the moral crisis of our times. [Duncan Williams, *The Trousered Ape* (New Rochelle: Arlington House, 1972), p.24.]

parody of it.* A perceptive critic observes that "The hipsters - and they resemble the beatniks in this respect - are too fiercely wedded to their subjectivity, their rebellious egotism, and their driving need for sexual expression, to have sufficient energy left for the concentrated labor of creation."[81]

Approaching the 1980s, the writers' revulsion with America becomes more subdued, their anger more muted, their political reference unfocused. They look at evil not so much as an individual or institutionalized phenomenon that can be located and exposed, but rather as an omnipresent and elusive system of untruths, conspiracies, or machinations, a new form of oppression permeating all spheres of life Espionage and various covert activities, or terrorist actions, become preferred metaphors of human reactions and relations. For some, the motif is not new. In the fictions of Mailer, Burroughs, or Pynchon, narrators claim that various conspiratorial or cancerous forces mysteriously control American life. What makes the 1980s and the early 1990s views of conspiracy different is that they treat it as widespread, on-going, virtually official, and an ultimately acceptable condition of life. Writer-heroes are exposed to it in the course of their narrations, they become its awed victims and avid explorers. Exley, the novelist in Frederick Exley's *Last Notes from Home* (1988), learns that people practice falsehood deliberately, make it their lifestyle or philosophy. For example, his brother, "the Brigadier," does not die of cancer, Exley discovers, but of the guilt he suffers for his work for the Military Intelligence in Vietnam, where he may have been involved in the My Lai atrocity. In Philip Roth's *Operation Shylock* (1993), the writer called Philip Roth is confronted by his look-alike, an ex-private detective who steals his name and credentials and uses them for

---

*Accused of inciting and romanticizing violence, of publicizing criminals (in 1981, he defends Jack Henry Abbott, a convicted killer who, having won an early release from prison, kills again), or just of presenting himself as a man of wild instincts, Mailer has not, as yet, published a novel about the life of a man-of-letters who is a hipster. The confusion of the material hidden underneath Mailer's vision of such a hero may be too immense, the task of dealing with it too complex or elusive, even for someone who has so eloquently fantasized about these themes. More likely, the concept of the writer as a radical and self-destructive nihilist is ultimately too abstract, or too contrary to the American grain, to be contained in literary form.

a fanatical political mission in Israel. When he tries to expose the fraud, he finds himself entangled in Mossad's undercover operation dealing with a massive conspiracy involving rich Jews in league with Jasser Arafat and the Palestinians.

John Barth's *Sabbatical* (1982) proposes that the American conspiracy inevitably involves the writer both as man and artist. A sense of impending danger haunts Fenwick Scott Key Turner, an aspiring novelist and his wife Susan, a professor of English, as they set out on a sea voyage. Shots are fired at night on an island which they are surprised to find unchartered, their own boat is shot at, a friend dies of a heart attack that may have been induced. Fenwick feels the CIA was behind these and other mysterious incidents. He is a former employee of the Agency. His novel about covert operations has strained relations with it. The Agency tries to persuade him to return; it also attempts to recruit members of his family. Fenwick considers himself a marked man. He feels his former colleagues may be responsible for his own recent heart attack. He and his wife fear that the conspiracies, spying, and Byzantine machinations of the CIA and like organizations are inevitably becoming standards for human relations. In their "shadowy world...the world of information, disinformation, even superdisinformed supercoded disinformation... simple truth and falsehood, fact and fiction, loyalty and disloyalty, may be as difficult to distinguish - indeed, may be as naive a distinction, as...uh...happiness and unhappiness, or love and less-than-love...."[82] Like Garp or Citrine, the Turners are deeply concerned about the state of their country and Western civilization in general. Both are, they feel, in a state of decay or entropy. They fear outside dangers: the proliferation of nuclear weapons, the cold war, the destruction of natural resources. They also feel that inside threats like the secret power of intelligence and military circles and the rising crime rate are becoming a new and particularly sinister mix. Their relatives and friends have been affected by it. Susan's twin, gangraped and beaten by a motorcycle gang, then raped again by the driver she asked for help, has given birth to a moronic child. Others have been victims, or witnesses of, sudden unexplained deaths, suicides, disappearances and other inexplicable events. Emotionally exhausted, Fenwick and Susan decide to search for a more satisfying existence. But their sabbatical, a sea-cruise and novel-writing journey, is informed by a conviction that America's "ubiquitous silliness and arrogant vulgarity" co-exist with life's plottings and conspiracies and that the resulting "reality of the irreality" fuses with various celebrated literary myths, Francis Scott Key, Edgar Allan Poe, a sea monster.[83] Creating "a modern version of the American romance novel," and "drawing on its twin traditions of terror and sentimentality," as Malcolm Bradbury phrases it, the Turners propose a belief that American reality is ominously cryptic and tangled, perpetually manipulated, increasingly dependent on clandestine processes and operations.[84] The contemporary writer, an alarmed and curious observer, tries to capture it in a manner that accentuates the vaguely mythical, the magical, the indeterminate, the heavily self-reflexive.

Joan Didion's *Democracy* (1984) focuses on a similar theme: the power of various government agencies and representatives linked with corporations and the criminal underworld to carry out covert operations purportedly connected with United States policy. The narrator, identified as Joan Didion, a baffled and wary gatherer of life's splintered meanings and disconnected images, is puzzled by the bluntness and zeal of her characters. Among them is Jack Lovett, a dapper man in his sixties, a former army officer and ostensibly a diplomat, who has "access to airplanes," conducts "a little business here and there," keeps "the usual balls in the air."[85] People know that this "war lover" stands for the shadow world of arms sales, political coups, and destabilization in all parts of the world, but no one questions him, and he never explains. He, like the people he deals with, tiresomely amasses intelligence, manipulates it, turns it into profit. The data are useful and politically purposeful, even "Inaccurate information is in itself accurate information about the informant." It takes people like Lovett, Didion comprehends, to know that "A Laotian village indicated on one map and omitted on another suggested not a reconnaissance oversight but a population annihilated, x number of men, women, and children lined up one morning between the maps and bulldozed into a common ditch."[86]

Other characters of *Democracy* are, like Lovett, sinister, pompous and haughty, desensitized to what happens around them. They act violently, or blandly, because they live in media-enhanced illusions in which individuals are shaped by a ceaseless flood of images, twisted and dulled reflections of a disjointed culture. Didion-the-character studies them over a period of many years, tries to make sense of the fragmented and lonely world around her, or, metaphorically, below her - she is like an aerialist who "knows that to look down is to fall," but who wants "to stay on the wire in this novel of fitful glimpses."[87]

Bill Gray, an aging, reclusive but respected novelist in Don DeLillo's *Mao II* (1991), is likewise an entranced observer of media manipulation, covert scheming and violence. As befits the age of the CNN, his experiences have global dimensions. Asked by his editor to speak out in behalf of a well-known poet taken hostage by terrorists in Beirut, Bill agrees to emerge from his self-imposed hermitage to give a public reading of the poet's work. When the reading is postponed because of a bomb threat, Bill finds himself drawn, by events, and by his own fascination with the workings of political coercion, into the world of Middle-Eastern terrorism. Fleeing his sponsors, he travels, on his own, to Athens, and then Beirut at the time when Lebanon is in turmoil. He expects to meet the terrorists who, he knows, will almost certainly take him hostage. Trance-like, he is drawn to meet those who like writers want to influence the society, to make an impact on it:

> There's a curious knot that binds novelists and terrorists. In the West we become famous effigies as our books lose the power to shape and influence....Years ago I used to think it was possible for a novelist to alter the inner life of the culture. Now bomb-makers and gunmen have taken that territory. They make raids on human consciousness.
>
> ....
>
> Because we're giving way to terror, to news of terror, to tape recorders and cameras, to bombs stashed in radios. News of disaster is the only narrative people need.[88]

The notion that America, even the whole of Western culture, can be seen as orchestrating a secret intrigue, or a terrorist plot, is communicated with full force already in the 1960s by several black American writers. John A. Williams' novel *The Man Who Cried I Am* (1967) is an example of a direct and extensive illustration of how the black writer viewed the claims of the country's racial integration as mere political manipulation and saw himself threatened by vast political intrigues and plottings. The novel's hero, Max Reddick, a Black American journalist and novelist, learns of the government's secret plan to remove the country's black leaders and dissidents to concentration camps in case of a large racial confrontation. Harry Ames, the man who hands him the document about the plan, is shot dead. The killers are black CIA agents who claim to be writers.

In Williams' *!Click Song* (1982), the black novelist William Cato Douglass, who tries to establish himself as a serious writer, is convinced that he, and black artists like him, are subjected to widespread bias and intrigues of white Americans, especially those in the publishing industry. He complains: "White writers were always running off to Africa, literally and fictionally, to mine for gold. My novels...hadn't even gone into paperback editions, and this was in a time when a good fart could bring fifty biggies without too much trouble." He sees his own successful university career as evidence of white duplicity towards blacks: "for the administration...I was...the showpiece nigger...a nigger who *writes*!" But Williams' view of the American system as an internal conspiracy goes here beyond racial lines. Americans across the board are its victims. Young people, for example, are to him "poorly educated, miseducated and/or *programmed* not to know very much about themselves, their nation or the world. The *plan* seemed to be to keep them precisely that way." (italics mine)[89]

Williams' work is something of a relic among recent novels by serious Afro-American novelists because its angry message is given a traditional form within a factual and conventional social and cultural environment. By the later 1970s and 1980s, Afro-American writers' visions of America as a conspiracy against them more typically turn into surreal, nervously absurd and fatalistically self-effacing jokes or gags, as Ishmael Reed's *Reckless Eyeballing* (1988) and other works demonstrate, or into obsessively bitter and ironic metaphors, as is the case with John Edgar Wideman's autobiographical *Brothers and Keepers* (1984). In both, images of writers are subordinated to the parodic exigencies of modern form, not to internal veracity. They are flattened by exaggeration, emptied by indiscriminate irony.

Characteristically, the writer-heroes of the past two decades, while declaring themselves repulsed by the deterioration of life in the United States, show an amazing aptitude to adjust to its manifest evils and conflicts. Their castigations of corruption, falsehood and intrigue provide an opportunity to explore the labyrinths of the postmodern psyche. They do not act so much as adversaries of the American order, but as more or less serious impersonators or manipulators of its deviant possibilities. They are not dissenters, but utilizers and exploiters of dissension. Their clashes with the American system leave them more strong-willed, more inured to its ironies and discords than they once were, capable of creating "correctives."[*] If they sound like the voice of native consciousness, it is because they refer to large issues and speak strongly about them. But their protestations are, by and large, short-lived and their criticism finally ineffectual.

THE UNDER TOAD IS STRONG IN EUROPE

Critics often stress the physically withdrawn, settled and self-centered qualities of both the contemporary author and his fictional representations. Yet the American writer is not necessarily an introvert or hermit - as Jerzy Kosinski calls his alter ego in his last novel. Many of them engage in outward experiences and possibilities, sometimes outside their own country.

---

[*]Josephine Hendin's term. In *Vulnerable People: A View of American Fiction Since 1945* (New York: Oxford University Press, 1978), she sees recent American fiction not as a record of "spiritual and emotional impoverishment," but evidence of "how we withstand them." "The changes in our fiction reflect changes in our adaptation to life." [*Vulnerable People*, p.4.]

Europe is the exotic territory they frequently explore. After World War II they often visit there semi-officially, as cultural-political missionaries. In 1958 Archibald MacLeish, poet, playwright, editor, himself a distinguished State Department cultural envoy abroad, wrote in *The Atlantic Monthly*:

> In Athens it was Bill Faulkner. In Paris it was Thornton Wilder. In London it was Robert Frost himself. You can say almost anything about the State Department these days but you can't say it isn't exporting the evidences of American culture.[90]

MacLeish was worried that foreign audiences would see his arguments as irrelevant, and himself as a symbol of American materialism. But writer-protagonists populating fiction after the 1960s experience more complex frustrations. And their itineraries are different from those MacLeish and his contemporaries or previous expatriate writers of this century followed. Rather than visiting France, Spain, or Italy, they travel to Germany - or they venture beyond the Iron Curtain, the final political frontier.

These parts of Europe become to many a writer-hero the territory where the various sinister and murky evils and villainous energies of the past can be traced beneath the reconstructions of order and democracy of Western Europe, or the drabness and political falsehood of the communist countries. A number of significant novels from John Hawkes' *The Cannibal* (1949), through Thomas Pynchon's *Gravity's Rainbow* (1973), to Kosinski's *The Hermit of 69th Street* focus on Germany as the heartland of some hidden quintessential villainy that is at the root, somehow, of mankind's postwar chaos. Characters speak of their revulsion for such dark heritage, but they also reveal a sense of curiosity about its workings and present day repercussions. Esther, the aspiring writer in Plath's *The Bell Jar*, tells us that her father "came from some manic-depressive hamlet in the black heart of Prussia." She at first hates the idea of learning German, but later finds herself willing to go to Germany, becoming bilingual.[91] Erica Jong's Isadora Wing, who has spent some time in Germany and speaks the country's language, is in "panic" whenever she goes back there. Germany is to her like a stepmother: "utterly familiar, utterly despised. More despised, in fact, for being so familiar." The country's cleanliness is only an illusion ("illusion, mind you, because Germans are really not clean"), "a carefully contrived facade to intimidate foreigners with Germany's aggressive wholesomeness." Airports, streets, faces of people make Isadora think of the wartime horrors. Even German toilets are to her "really the key to the horrors of the Third Reich. People who can build toilets like this are capable of anything."[92]

When Ulrich Hargenau, a writer who lives in Paris, in Walter Abish's *How German Is It* (1980), visits Germany (where his father was executed for plotting against Hitler) so as to learn about its contemporary character, he is badly frightened. Is it merely "a fear left over from another period," a cheap stereotype that "represents nothing but a deeply buried desire to retain the image of the Germans as collectively dangerous and destructive, bent on destroying and eradicating anything that might remotely be considered a threat to their existence."[93] What he sees sustains his apprehension, resurrects the country's grim past. Where there was once a large concentration camp with the obligatory train tracks connection that makes one think of "an occasional scarecrow face framed in the tiny cutout window of a freight car," there is a new urban center for well-educated, successful middle-class citizens who want to be "closer to the countryside and live in a community with better schools and fewer foreigners and new job opportunities."[94] Germany's effort to rebuild the country camouflages a deeper need to erase its past, to eradicate its memory, to replace it with modern comfort and functionality. To forget, in fact, that the war had taken place. Helmut, Urlich's brother, a gifted, energetic architect and a model of enterprising efficiency and a relentless master builder of a new Germany, is to Ulrich an example of a perfect counterfeiter of history, as is Brumhold, the celebrated German philosopher who would like to re-capture the essence of Germany by embracing the countryside's primeval soul "rooted in the rich dark soil of *der Schwarzwald.*"[95]

Raymond Federman's heroes also detect a sense of deep-rooted evil in the

German psyche, but they do not formulate it with a mixture of suppositions and doubts, as Abish does, which the very title of his work suggests. In *The Twofold Vibration* an old writer whose parents had been murdered by the Nazis, takes a wild and impulsive trip to Germany to see Wagner's *Parsifal*, but finds the opera to be an inspiration for "Hitler's hysterical Hollywoodian spectacles." The Germans adore its "mysticopolitical masquerades" and its images of power, "cunningly phantasmagorial and tragically self-destructive." It appeals to their hidden sense of "social hypocrisy and brutalization." "Dangerously rich and complacent," they know how to hide behind orderly disguises and well-organized exteriors.[96] On a visit to Dachau the writer finds it hard to "get to the core of this thing," the horror of the past. He fears the truth of evil will be removed, covered up. The neatness of the camp reminds him of the Ford Museum near Detroit, but instead of culminating in some final outcome, like the "beautiful shiny latest model of Ford," it leads to "vacuum...nothing...an absence...death." Disturbed about his experiences in Germany, this "double-headed monster of duplicity," upset by his failure to win money at a casino, "to leave this fucking country rich," the old writer attempts to take his life. But the chandelier in his Baden-Baden hotel disproves his conceit that "anything German is solid." Lying among the debris of the ceiling, mortified by onlookers who "stared at me with their German gaze," he angrily realizes he cannot "even die in this fucking country."[97]

In *Mother Night* (1961), Vonnegut recognizes the evils rooted in war-time Germany through the writer called Howard Campbell. This "Nazi by reputation" acquainted with the higher circles of the war-time Germany (Rudolf Hoess confessed to him at a party in Warsaw that he had "some marvelous stories to tell"), thinks of his role in wartime Germany in terms defined by Goethe's Mephistopheles: "a part of the part that at first was all, part of the darkness...Mother Night," a stage that preceded civilization's trivial and treacherous epoch of "supercilious light."[98] Life in postwar United States, Campbell speculates, is an extension of Mother Night. It is "that simple and widespread boon to modern mankind - schizophrenia."[99]

In *Slaughterhouse-Five* (1969), the Vonnegut persona similarly uses his past and present stays in Germany, where "the greatest massacre in European history, which was the fire-bombing of Dresden" took place, to extrapolate about the state of America in the 1960s.[100] War crimes (an obvious allusion to Vietnam) are committed by bureaucrats, military scientists, historians, propagandists. They are largely responsible for the insanity, absurdity and violence that pervade American reality long after the end of World War II. Like Campbell, Vonnegut and Billy Pilgrim proclaim that the postwar reality paralyzes them, make them unable to deal with the meanings of the war, and consequently of life in general.

Themes of Europe's wartime horrors are foregrounded in the North American psyche at the time when, in 1947, it was not ready for them, in William Styron's *Sophie's Choice* (1979). Stingo, an aspiring Southern writer resembling the Styron of the early postwar years, comes to New York City to attain sexual fulfillment and artistic achievement, but is confronted with the tales of Sophie, a young and beautiful Polish woman who experienced the war and Auschwitz, "that fetid sinkhole of her past." Her testimony astounds rather than horrifies him, or affects him artistically. It will take him many years to realize that her ghoulish revelations have been at the bottom of the moral-philosophical crisis of his times. In the voice of the older, artistically mature Stingo, Styron reflects on how perplexing moral issues must have been, how wrenching the choices, if allowed to be taken, how devastating the related guilt and redemption of people who have lived through the Holocaust. The psychological depth-analysis of the executors of Auschwitz he undertakes - though he recognizes he is merely an "intruder upon the terrain of an experience so bestial, so inexplicable, so undetachably and rightfully the possession alone of those who suffered and died, or survived it" - points to an emergence of a new and peculiarly inhuman sense of moral void in Germany, one that has become a "consummate travesty" of that country's scientific "efflorescence" of the 19th century. Rudolf Höss was "hardly a sadist, nor was he a violent man," rather a "servomechanism in which a moral vacuum had been so successfully sucked clean of every molecule of real qualm or scruple that his own descriptions of the unutterable crimes he perpetrated daily seem often to float outside and apart from evil, phantasms of cretinous innocence."[101]

Kosinski's protagonists, though aware of the corrupt nature of mankind in general, carry with them what seems like an acute, all-controlling remembrance of Germany's wartime atrocities, which they themselves experienced in various parts of Europe. Their minds are never free of the responsibility to keep the Nazi evil continually exposed and condemned. The novelist in *The Hermit of 69th Street* is outraged by anyone who tries to diminish the unique viciousness of Germany under Hitler. He feels that fear and superstition, a metaphysical condition buried deep in the German soul, unleashed a new quality of inhumanity and primitivism upon the consciousness of our times. His comment on Hannah Arendt's account of Eichmann's trial takes the form of a ferocious moral-social-historical diatribe:

> Were these peasants, these Slavic folks more superstitious or less so than your CIVILIZED heel-clicking, oh-so-obedient GERMANS WHO BELIEVED IN A HIDDEN DEVIL - A DEVIL HIDDEN IN EVERY JEW? The fact is...I would rather kiss every day the dirty feet of any Ruthenian peasant than ever again salute anything militaristically German and this goes for any Jewish intellectual Dragon Lady like you. Am I clear? Is it said enough? Not enough![102]

John Irving's heroes detect the Old World's inhumanity and grimness south of Germany, in Vienna. Garp, in *The World According to Garp*, feels that the city, in the sixties still healing the wounds of the war and the Russian occupation, its people, culture and history, has a "death phase," or "a cadaver" quality about it.

> All around Garp the city looked ripe with dying. The teeming parks and gardens reeked of decay to him, and the subject of the great painters in the great museums was always death.[103]

Seen from the perspective of Vienna, "all Europe, maybe, was a dressed up corpse in an open coffin."[104] It is here, among the depravations of the Old World, however, that Garp, and various other Irving heroes, see their mature life begin to take place. Here they gain experience and artistic maturity, and both are filled with the recognition of the universal nature of raw aggression. Garp's first story in Austria is haunted by the themes of death and violence. When he visits the country again, many years later, now the author of a notorious novel, which reviewers see as "paranoid, crazed, and crammed with gratuitous violence and sex," Vienna, already a content and prosperous city, is to him, like the Germany Ulrich Hargenau experiences, both filled with "something new but common" and redolent of the gloom and danger of the past, a place where, Garp feels, "the Under Toad was strong."[105]

In the 1960s travel restrictions to countries behind the Iron Curtain were eased, and Moscow, Prague, Warsaw, and other centers of communist rule become available to American writers, artists, and intellectuals. During the next three decades they travel there as America's ambassadors of culture and good will, as university exchange lecturers, as guests of various cultural institutions, or as tourists. Once inside these countries they discover that the "other Europe" proves to be full of unexpected complexities and absurdities, while they themselves become strangely unnerved by it, ill-at-ease, comically exposed, bewildered.

Henry Bech, in John Updike's *Bech: A Book* (1970), is sent to Moscow in 1964 as "an ambassador of the arts." Here he is treated as a V.I.P. and, "just once in his life," has more money than he can manage to spend.[106] Besides a sumptuous hotel, limousine service and a guide, he is given rubles to the value of fifteen hundred dollars ("in the guise of 'royalties'") for one of his novels published in a Russian edition of one hundred thousand copies. With nothing to buy in the country, he is unable to spend the money, yet the experience reveals a side of him that he finds puzzling and embarrassing. He sees himself becoming ostentatious, developing "a clowning super-American manner that disguised all complaints as 'acts.'" His guide and interpreter reprimands him, in all seriousness, that he must not joke: "This is your money. You earned it by the sweat of your brain." In response, Bech scatters a wad of banknotes above his head and onto the rich red carpet of the hotel. When she suggests that he put the money in the bank, he exclaims: "No Kate, we must spend it! Spend, spend. It's the Keynesian way. We will make mother Russia a consumer society." On another occasion, when stopped in the street by a stranger who wants to buy his overcoat, or shoes, Bech, by comic reversal, pulls out his wallet and offers the man fifty dollars for *his* shoes. Offended by his buffoonery, Kate tells him he treats her country "as a picnic," while Bech, aware of his nervous and crude patronizing, feels "especially sick and guilty."[107]

Throughout the remainder of his tour of communist Europe, Bech confronts several similar manifestations of his own brusqueness and social incompetence, of the failure to explore interesting possibilities and to make friendships. In Bulgaria, for example, where he meets a poetess, Vera Glavanakova, to him the embodiment of a "central woman," he again sees himself acting foolishly and falsely. He explains to her the patterns of his own fiction in terms that are conspicuously "contrived," as if it were a "quixotically complex experiment," and not a "failure" at the bottom of which, Bech suspects, was his own "simple laziness." Ashamed of his inauthentic role, he feels "a secret intoxication and a secret guilt."[108]

In similar fashion, Philip Roth's characters, who come to Czechoslovakia to pursue various literary and spiritual goals, observe other people's alienation or corruption as well as their own lack of judgment, disillusionment, irrelevance. One of them, the novelist Nathan Zuckerman, in *The Prague Orgy* (1985), discovers that the artists and intellectuals he meets in Prague, though eccentric and demoralized, appear oddly attractive to him because out of their "unbearable condition" they seem to be making out a "witty, stylish comedy of manners" that is in contrast with his "dignified, well-behaved, reliable spectator, secure, urbane, calm, polite" deportment.[109] Their political discussions are ongoing, deftly self-censored, acts of survival; their explicit sexual games turn into political demonstrations, while their humor is a form of self-defense. Overwhelmed by such intellectual exuberance, Zuckerman feels that, although rich and acclaimed in his own country, he lacks the fierce glamour of Prague's beleaguered and picturesque intellectuals. His personal involvement seems small and uncertain, while his efforts to salvage some important Yiddish stories fail. His search for the historical Kafka is in vain because, as someone tells him, "Kafka is dead."[110]

In Roth's more recent *Deception* (1990), the writer-narrator called Philip meets Czech and Polish refugees in London. He listens sympathetically to their confessional accounts of life under oppression and tells them he understands their guilt and confusion. He remembers, and is remembered, visiting Prague in the 1970s and meeting writers and students, being harassed and arrested by the police and leaving Czechoslovakia as *persona non grata*. Yet when asked about "all that Czechoslovak mirroring of everything...", he says "I'm not sure what it adds up to, if anything." On another occasion he says he has been to Czechoslovakia "for the jokes."[111] The themes of political oppression along with the absurdities of the communist system, though at once stimulating and confounding, are finally too remote and confusing for him. Like Roth's other fictional visitors to Czechoslovakia, like Roth himself, as he expressed it in interviews, Philip treats politics mainly as background for his own comic and animated reconstructions of Europe, or for effective aesthetic analogies.

Judith Horne, an American culture critic and a successful writer, a participant at an international conference on American culture held in Warsaw in 1980, in Joyce Carol Oates's "My Warszawa" (1981, collected in *Last Days*, 1984), finds her brief stay in the increasingly tense Poland peculiarly unnerving, an experience that reveals her progressive loss of confidence and self-control. This "thoroughly successful woman," as she sees herself, who "has travelled widely since the age of twenty," whose name is "comfortably *known*," whose lecture tours and publications bring her "a steady income," feels "she isn't herself" in Warsaw:

> Judith cannot tell them that she feels unreal; a fiction, an imposter;...She feels weak. She feels Jewish at last. And womanly - in the very worst sense of the word.

A Jew, a woman, a victim - can it be?[112]

Judith's ethnic background, and her sense of herself as a woman, the two issues about which she is sensitive and the subject of much public curiosity, become the joint territory of her mental crisis in Poland. She comes to realize she is a fragile character, filled with bitterness and self-hatred, unable to comprehend herself, let alone the complexity of the foreign culture she is trying to penetrate. She wonders "which direction her emotions might rush next," finds herself beset by situations and sights she detests: cigarette smoke in public places, shoddy goods in stores, long queues.[113] The outer clashes with the inner, the public with the personal, the need to be in control with the need to be loved. Her war with herself parallels what she sees as Poland's internal conflicts: home to both Communism and Catholicism, victim and oppressor. The views of Warsaw like the Old Town District, restored from ruins after the war, move her deeply, but also create more emotional disorientation. When people around her speak of the country's tragic past and painful present, she uncovers evidence of hypocrisy and anti-Semitism. The figures on the monument of the Jewish Ghetto lack Jewish features. No one is able to tell her how many Jews still live in Poland. Most tellingly, her obviously Jewish interviewer renounces her past and her identity.

The characters discussed above are doubtless glib and superficial in their collective responses to communist Europe. To them, the daily patter of persecution and humiliation are unreal and absurd - an incompatible and distorted counterpart to life in the West. Thus, Updike's Henry Bech feels that he moves over the landscapes of the "other half of the world, the hostile mysterious half," without needing to engage, or to fully acknowledge this alien world; he admits finally that his East-European "errands" are useless and "ridiculous."[114] He sees the people of the Soviet Union, Rumania, or Bulgaria as a distant and strangely twisted species, a "people behind the mirror."[115] Observing the flamboyant intellectuals in *The Prague Orgy*, Zuckerman muses: "They, silenced, are all mouth. I am only ears - and plans, an American gentleman abroad, with the bracing if old-fashioned illusion that he is playing a worthwhile, dignified, an honorable role."[116] "Why am I here," muses Judith Horne looking at the street map of Warsaw, "why in this room, in this city...?".[117] Warsaw, this "particular place," is to her "an occupied city, an occupied zone," a place that seems to be filled with poison, "[t]he place", Judith thinks, "of my undoing." Carl Walser, a journalist friend working on a story about Poland, comforts her: "East Europe is a strain on anyone's nerves."[118]

None of these characters makes any sustained attempt to comprehend the deeper cultural or artistic significance of the countries they visit, or to study the psychological qualities of people suppressed by communism. They also fail to reveal how their brief uneasy encounters with "the other Europe" help them think of their country, or face it on their return. Patricia Hampl's memoir *A Romantic Education* (1981), which addresses a young woman's fascination with Czechoslovakia in the 1970s, offers more in that respect. During her first stay in Prague, in 1975, Hampl feels as if she has entered her parents' Depression era, "the ruined quality." "I was, simply, in the most beautiful place I had ever seen, and it was grimy and sad and broken." Czechoslovakia, to her the heart of Europe, reveals itself as "the sadness of the continent." But she likes the fusion of disarray and intricacy and feels it stands for a truer culture than her own. Back in the States, she finds herself perturbed by people's lack of cultivation, their complacency and "misdirected" energy. She sees Americans as "utopians, in search of an *idea* because there wasn't the finer satisfaction of a culture."[119]

Her second visit to Prague, two years later, turns the bitterness into a theory. Hampl feels that the "significance of Czechoslovakia" is linked to the West's haunted quality of grief and consequently to "the curious emptiness that has been the subject of Western literature at least since the Second World War, perhaps since the First World War."[120] One of the forgotten causes of the present anxiety, she reasons, is the 17th century destruction of the magical, or alchemical, tradition of which Prague was the historical capital. "Exactly here, one might say, at the Battle of the White Mountain near Prague, is one of the places where science and religion were broken apart from each other, wounding Western consciousness profoundly." Consequently the Renaissance was divested of its magical tradition, mechanical science superseded philosophy and lead to "the split of consciousness with which we continue to live." It filled the Western world with fear, especially the fear of mystery, a condition which "has justified every atrocity in our immediate history."[121]

Though clearly pleased with her ability to mix American sensibilities with insights into Eastern Europe, also far from declaring herself defeated by the life of Czechoslovakia, Hampl sees her own functioning there much like the characters of Updike, Roth, or Oates. She goes to Czechoslovakia naively hoping to find instant confirmation of political malevolence, a cohesive past, a sense of purity. Like Roth's heroes, she assumes that the physical and mental traces of Kafka in Prague can provide a key to layers of forgotten historical-literary sensibility, but finds them to be a tangle of elusive, all-purpose cultural epigrams. Confused and disappointed, yet enthralled by the grimness, the sadness, "the broken beauty of the city," she acknowledges the fragility of American perceptions and experiences a sense of fatigue and apprehension. The sight of a policeman observing her as she tries to open the lock to a friend's house fills her with terror, "the terror of strangeness, the knowledge that couldn't be kept off any longer that I didn't know anything in this crazy misty city I kept trying to claim."[122] She comes to realize Prague is not like "Paris or London - there is no way for an ordinary American to live here." Looking back at her earlier fascination with things Czechoslovak, she admits she was deluded: "As a young American aggrieved by the Vietnam War, I suppose I wasn't, after all, looking for history, but for that more dangerous elixir: purity." She now wants to withdraw, to make Prague, the whole country, "to blur over and fade away."[123]

Although she ultimately returns to Czechoslovakia, shortly after the "velvet revolution," in order to experience the ongoing transformations, which she sees as being good and bad, admirable and kitschy, Hampl again accepts that the realities of this part of Europe, though now easily accessible, cannot be easily understood.[*] She suggests that they challenge the American observer, who is full of fear that he has lost a satisfying relationship with history. As a young girl, she noticed that her family had "no sense of history"; her grandmother did not even know the name of the village she had come from. It was the old woman's photographs of "Golden Prague" that made her realize she was going to be mysteriously reliant on Europe, hungry for its culture and its layers of history, eager to "make something out of what my family says is nothing." Convinced of her latent literary talent, she hoped her "ache" for history could be "assuaged by an act of the imagination."[124] Later she learned that a loss of history was not her exclusive concern. Americans in general suffer because they have exempted themselves from a dialogue with the past. "We are haunted by history because we denied its reality when it was present" - and now must somehow try to regain it, "get the story straight."[125]

The heroine of "My Warszawa," though scornful of "personal hungers with grandiose 'historical' notions," similarly feels that in her country "history is something that happened only a few weeks ago - or didn't happen."[126] Both women, much like the other writer-characters discussed here, go to Eastern Europe with the desire to reclaim a vision of the past, or a pattern of history with which they could identify or relate to. Unable to attain such goals, uncomfortable with the versions of history they find, they become disenchanted - or ironic. Though Hampl knows that "it is really the longing for a lost culture that sends Americans on these pilgrimages," she inevitably comes to appreciate her country's loss of history. "History, for people like me...begins in America....Europe is an opaque historylessness, full of towns we can't pronounce and languages we will never speak."[127]

American assimilation of European history, like pilgrimages made routinely by her countrymen, is, Judith Horne thinks, superficial and grotesquely naive. Members of an American delegation of "cultural emissaries," whom she meets in

---

[*]Hampl's views of the post-revolutionary Prague of 1991 are contained in an Afterward in the 1992 edition.

Warsaw, speak of having absorbed "firsthand the tragic history of Poland...Hungary ...Bulgaria, Yugoslavia and Czechoslovakia" and expect to be similarly enlightened by a visit to East Germany. Her own view of Poland's history, Judith suspects, is based on stereotypes as outdated and unrelated to its present realities as the prose of Henry James (Judith takes with her a copy of *The Awkward Age*) because "she has brought to this beleaguered country hazy but stubborn ideas about 'people' and their integrity." Poles themselves are, according to her, a tragically confused people, some of them "don't even know their own history."[128]

At the end of his stay in Rumania, Updike's Bech feels "a vengeful satisfaction and glad sense of release." He realizes "that for four days he had been afraid."[129] Arrested by the police and forced to leave Czechoslovakia, seeing that "the dangers were real" indeed, Zuckerman is glad to be able to disassociate himself from the world which, in the past, his own "fortunate family had eluded." He dreads the thought he might have to live in a country where a writer may be reduced to "a sweeper of floors in a railway café."[130] Judith Horne views life in Poland with apprehension: "[she] tries not to think: censorship, repression, contempt for women, anti-Semitism, pogroms. Yes there have always been pogroms...."[131] Hampl discovers that Czechoslovakia "had little, after all, to do with me."[132] Fearing that the ghosts of the past which loom amongst the daily realities of the communist world are too grimly unreal and complex to be contained, all these characters, like Bellow's Henderson, come to resent the difficulty and complexity of their once purposeful journeys and are happy to return to the absurdities and unrealities of the life with which they are familiar.

All these European confessions of the American writer-hero are grounded in vexed and conflicting emotions. They oscillate between a passion for exploring unknown territories, or new relationships, and a compulsion to renounce foreign experiences, between the love of historical heritage and a wayward suspicion of it.*

---

*A contradiction which Leon Botstein defines as a "peculiar symbiosis between nostalgia and de-historicization" and calls one of American fiction's new dominant features. ["...and an absent rigour," *The Times Literary Supplement*, Sept.15-21, 1989.]

They reveal a new and peculiarly mythic perception of Europe. The Old World is no longer compared to the New, as James understood it, or seen as a refuge where new psychological or artistic temptations, or creative withdrawals, can be absorbed, as the whole generation of American artists and intellectuals in the Twenties wanted to practice it.* Instead, it becomes a territory where the evidence, both mental and physical, of our civilization's darker instincts can be located. Its somber history, its dilemmas and paradoxes serve the writer as material for personal soul-searching, temporary refuge, or for an imaginative re-working. Europe serves as a useful excavation ground in which the origins of the Western culture can be traced, a handy reference file for pondering America's present historical-cultural dissolution. Europe's problems, its cultural richness and historical complexity, its war horrors, its cultural-political predicament in countries dominated by the communist system are not important as facts, or social or cultural truths, but as useful signs and symbols of an ancient heritage of human potential and failure. Writer-heroes visit Europe expecting to find in it a convenient mixture of the historical and the sinister, the absurd and the grim, to be animated by mankind's deep-seated hunger for savagery and dominance. Confronted with unexpected complex realities, imagining that they themselves might have been a part of what they see as the dark historical or political evils rooted in these places, they are faced with their own uneasiness or stupefaction, a sense of repulsion and the inevitable need to withdraw.

---

*Reassessing the literary travels and exiles of those years, Thomas Wolfe states in his autobiographical *The Story of a Novel* (1936) that the attractiveness of Europe was not in what Americans in the 1920s expected to find there in the first place. What they were really trying to do was to leave behind "not the Philistinism, the materialism, and ugliness in American life," but "the necessity of grappling squarely with ourselves and the necessity of finding in ourselves, somehow, the stuff to live by, to get from our own lives and our own experience the substance of our art which every man who ever wrote a living thing has had to get out of himself and without which he is lost." [Thomas Wolfe, *The Story of a Novel* (New York: Scribner's, 1936), p.29.]

NOTES

1.William H. Gass, *In the Heart of the Heart of the Country*, p.193.

2.Tom Wolfe, *The Electric Kool-Aid Acid Test*, p.190.

3.Kurt Vonnegut, *Mother Night*, p.29.

4.Gilbert Sorrentino, *Mulligan Stew*, p.22.

5.John A. Williams, *Click Song* (New York: Thunder Mouth Press, 1987), p.341.

6.Ronald Sukenick, *Up*, p.328.

7.Ibid., pp.244-45.

8.Bernard Malamud, *The Tenants* (1971; Harmondsworth: Penguin, 1972), pp.12, 9.

9.Bernard Malamud, *Dubin's Lives*, pp.8-9, 141, 161.

10.Saul Bellow, *Humboldt's Gift*, p.69.

11.Sanford Pinsker, "Literature," *American Quarterly*, ##1 and 2, Spring/Summer 1983, p. 120.

12.Saul Bellow, *Humboldt's Gift*, p.35.

13.Saul Bellow, *Herzog*, p.201.

14.Norbert Blei, *The Second Novel; Becoming a Writer* (Chicago: December Press, 1978), pp.79-80.

15.Ibid., p.79.

16.John Updike, *Bech is Back* (1982, New York: Fawcett Crest, 1983), p.112.

17.Capote, *Answered Prayers* (1987; London; Abacus, 1988), p.8.

18.Jerzy Kosinski, *The Hermit of 69th Street*, p.353-54.

19.Alfred Kazin, "New York: The Writer in the Powerhouse," *The New York Review*, October 10, 1985.

20.Truman Capote, *Answered Prayers*, pp.8-9.

21.Paul Theroux, "Lady Max," *Granta*, London, #40, Summer 1992, p.158.

22.Kenneth S. Lynn, "Adulthood in American Literature," *Daedalus*, Fall, 1976, also Summer, 1988.

23.Josephine Hendin, "The Writer as Culture Hero, The Father as Son," *Harper's*, July 1974.

24.Philip Roth, *The Anatomy Lesson* (1983; New York: Fawcett Crest, 1984), p.8.

25.Jack Kerouac, *On the Road*, p.5.

26.William H. Gass, *In the Heart of the Heart of the Country*, p.xxviii.

27.William Gass, *Willie Master's Lonesome Wife*, no page numbering.

28.Norbert Blei, *The Second Novel: Becoming a Writer*, p.3.

132

29.John Barth, *Lost in the Funhouse* (New York: Doubleday, 1968), p.85.

30.John Barth, *Chimera* (New York: Random House, 1972), pp. 24-25.

31.John Barth, *Sabbatical*, p.301.

32.John Barth, *The Tidewater Tales: A Novel* (New York: Putnam, 1987), p.114.

33.Philip Roth, *My Life as a Man*, pp.194-95.

34.Saul Bellow, *Humboldt's Gift*, pp.42, 219.

35.John Holmes, *Go*, p.33.

36.Norman Mailer, *Advertisements for Myself*, p.160.

37.Ernest Hemingway, *The Garden of Eden* (New York: Scribner's, 1986), p.29.

38.Jerzy Kosinski, *The Hermit of 69th Street*, p.52.

39.Paul Theroux, "Lady Max," pp.147-48, 158.

40.Paul Theroux, *My Secret History* (New York: Putnam's Sons, 1989), pp.169, 410.

41.Ibid., pp.463-65.

42.Philip Roth, *Zuckerman Unbound* (1981; Harmondsworth: Penguin, 1983), pp.55-57.

43.Bernard Malamud, *Dubin's Lives* (1978; New York: Avon, 1980), pp.10, 21.

44.Ibid., p.132.

45.Ibid., p.355.

46.Ibid., pp.385-86.

47.Philip Roth, *The Anatomy Lesson*, p.123.

48.Raymond Federman, *The Twofold Vibration*, p.73.

49.Ronald Sukenick, *Up*, p.280.

50.Ronald Sukenick, *Out*, p.82.

51.Jerzy Kosinski, *The Hermit of 69th Street*, p.336.

52.Norman Mailer, *Tough Guys Don't Dance* (London: Sphere Books, 1984), p. 37.

53.Gilbert Sorrentino, *Mulligan Stew*, p. 224.

54.Ibid., p.385.

55.Philip Roth, *The Counterlife*, pp.318-19.

56.Philip Roth, *The Facts*, p.191.

57.Philip Roth, *Deception*, p.95.

58.Erica Jong, *How to Save Your Own Life* (1977; New York: Signet, 1978), p.11.

59.Erica Jong, *Fear of Flying* (1973; New York: Signet, 1974), p.10.

60.Nathaniel Hawthorne, *The Scarlet Letter* (New York: Dodd, Mead and Company, 1948), p.35.

61.Sorrentino, Gilbert, *Splendide-Hôtel*, p.9.

62.John Updike, *Bech a Book*, p.VI.

63.Philip Roth, *My Life as a Man*, p.195.

64.John Barth, *Sabbatical*, p.225.

65.Joseph Heller, *Good As Gold* (1979; New York: Pocket Books, 1980), p.355.

66.Norman Mailer, *The Armies of the Night*, p.63.

67.Kurt Vonnegut, *Breakfast of Champions*, pp.5-12.

68.Kurt Vonnegut, *Slaughterhouse-Five*, p. 210.

69.Saul Bellow, *Humboldt's Gift* (New York: Viking, 1975), p.90.

70.Ibid., p.227.

71.Ibid., p.306.

72.John Irving, *The World According to Garp*, p.414.

73.Joyce Carol Oates, "My Warszawa," in *Last Days* (London: Jonathan Cape, 1985), p.140.

74.Truman Capote, *Answered Prayers* (1987, London: Abacus, 1988), pp.136-37.

75.Kurt Vonnegut, *Breakfast of Champions*, p.293.

76.Norman Mailer, *The Armies of the Night*, p. 320.

77.Norman Mailer, *Advertisements for Myself*, p.18.

78.Saul Bellow, *Humboldt's Gift*, p.43.

79.John Irving, *The World According to Garp"*, p.338-39.

80.Norman Mailer, *Tough Guys Don't Dance*, pp. 25, 102.

81.Charles I. Glicksberg, Martinus Nijhoff, *The Sexual Revolution in Modern American Literature* (The Hague, 1971), p.173.

82.John Barth, *Sabbatical*, p.93.

83.Ibid., pp. 298, 111.

84.Malcolm Bradbury, *The Modern American Novel* (1983; Oxford: Oxford University Press, 1984), p.182.

85.Joan Didion, *Democracy*, pp.31, 39.

86.Ibid., pp.36-37.

87.Ibid., pp.108, 232.

88.Don DeLillo, *Mao II* (1991; New York: Penguin, 1992), pp.41-42.

89.John A. Williams, *!Click Song* (1982; New York: Thunder Mouth Press, 1987), p.280-81, 298-99.

90. "The Isolation of the American Artist," Archibald MacLeish, *The Atlantic Monthly*, January 1958.

91.Sylvia Plath, *The Bell Jar*, p.34.

92.Erica Jong, *Fear of Flying* (1973, New York: Signet, 1974), pp.21-23.

93.Walter Abish, *How German Is It* (New York: New Directions, 1980), p.4.

94.Ibid., pp.78-79.

95.Ibid., p.5.

96.Raymond Federman, *The Twofold Vibration* (Bloomington: Indiana University Press, 1982), pp.77-83.

97.Ibid., pp.99-111.

98.Kurt Vonnegut, *Mother Night*, pp.xi, 17-26.

99.Ibid., p.133.

100.Kurt Vonnegut, *Slaughterhouse-Five*, p.101.

101.William Styron, *Sophie's Choice* (1979; New York: Bantam, 1980), pp.264-65, 179-180.

102.Jerzy Kosinski, *The Hermit of 69th Street*, p.524.

103.John Irving, *The World According to Garp*, p.116.

104.Ibid., p.117.

105.Ibid., pp.341-42.

106.John Updike, *Bech: A Book* (1970; Greenwich, Conn.: Fawcett Crest Book), 1971, pp.64, 16.

107.Ibid., pp.19-26.

108.Ibid., pp. 73, 82.

109.Philip Roth, *The Prague Orgy*, in *Zuckerman Bound* (New York: Farrar, Straus, Giroux, 1985), p.734-35.

110.Ibid., p.727.

111.Philip Roth, *Deception* (New York: Simon and Schuster, 1990), pp.189, 143.

112.Joyce Carol Oates, "My Warszawa," in *Last Days* (1984; London: Jonathan Cape, 1985), pp.159, 147-48.

113.Ibid., p.149.

114.John Updike, *Bech; A Book*, pp.64, 67.

115.Ibid., p. 82.

116.Philip Roth, *The Prague Orgy*, p.735.

117.Joyce Carol Oates, "My Warszawa," pp.167, 163, 146.

118.Ibid., pp.146-47.

119.Patricia Hampl, *A Romantic Education*, (Boston: Houghton Mifflin Company, 1981), p.151, 171, 203, 172.

120.Ibid., p.175.

121.Ibid., pp.218-19.

122.Ibid., pp.171, 298.

123.Ibid., pp.306-11.

124.Ibid., pp.9, 23.

125.Ibid., pp.251-52.

126.Joyce Carol Oates, "My Warszawa," pp.162, 157.

127.Patricia Hampl, *A Romantic Education*, pp.148, 164.

128.Joyce Carol Oates, "My Warszawa," pp.178, 137, 167.

129.John Updike, *Bech: A Book*, p.62.

130.Philip Roth, *The Prague Orgy*, pp.774, 778.

131.Joyce Carol Oates, "My Warszawa," p.152.

132.Patricia Hampl, *A Romantic Education*, p.164.

CHAPTER THREE

THE PAIN OF WRITING,
THE FAILURE OF SUCCESS

THE HARDSHIPS OF WRITING ENDURE

In *The Facts*, Zuckerman, the writer-protagonist, levels a barrage of accusations against Philip Roth, his creator and the book's autobiographical narrator. One of them is particularly urgent:

> Who are we, anyway? And why? Your autobiography doesn't tell us anything
> of what has happened, in your life, that has brought *us* out of you. There is
> an enormous silence about all that....What's the relation between this fiction
> and your present factuality?[1]

Here, Roth playfully acknowledges that a lack of connectedness between the writer's story and its birth, between literary statement and intellectual endeavor, is a noticeable weakness of fiction about writers. Indeed, the tradition of revealing oneself as an artist, an experimenter, a witness to struggle and failure, elation and loneliness, from Freneau through James to Ernest Hemingway, is largely non-existent in current American fiction. Rather than discuss the traditions of literary thought, or various ideas, as they shape the mind and life of the writer, as in, for example, Howells or James, or as in Sartre, Butor, Mauriac, Murdoch, Lessing and a number of other European authors, the recent American writer-hero prefers to explain outside circumstances of life in experimental and existential, as opposed to intellectual or artistic, terms. Even in the mode of postmodernism, which by its very nature is self-reflexive, he prefers to deal with the literature-making process rather than personal creative effort.

Critics[*] argue that, although the writer-hero occurs frequently in both nineteenth and early twentieth century American fiction, the history of his intellectual concerns has never been rich. The novel of the last twenty or thirty years moves the writing protagonist even farther away from the topic. Without precedent, he now speaks of the hypothetical nature of his own artistic experience, of the questionable character of the medium he executes, of the fear that, as Ambrose of Barth's *Lost in the Funhouse* observes, literature is "moribund if not already dead."[2] He similarly refuses to see writing fiction as a socially meaningful occupation.

Nevertheless a recurring theme probes the writer's perennial dilemma: anxiety concerning his ability to create characters, address unifying ideas, avoid distractions. Unlike his post-World War II predecessors, who felt numb in the changed world of the 1950s, the current writer-hero is fully aware that fiction can be imaginatively reworked to suit the views of modern experience. Yet he continues to complain that he is troubled by writing blocks, prolonged artistic silences and absences of creativity, that his work may be aborted, denied, deferred. He implies, or even openly declares, that he suffers because such failings deprive him of success.

Henry Bech, the novelist in John Updike's *Bech: A Book* (1970), and in *Bech is Back* (1982), relates a well-known tale. His early novels gained him a considerable reputation, with translations into several languages, as well as publication in anthologies, but his later work becomes hopelessly stalled.[**] He is unable to

---

[*]Philip Rahv, for example, deplores the poverty of the cerebral tradition in American letters and claims that the intellectual is the "only character missing in the American novel." Even Henry James is seen by Rahv as an artist basically dedicated to "the cult of experience." [Philip Rahv, *Image and Idea* (Norfolk, Connecticut: New Directions, 1949), p.9.]

[**]In a metafictional letter to Updike, in the foreword to *Bech: A Book*, Bech recognizes himself as an amalgam of writers like Mailer, Bellow, Roth, Malamud, or Singer, a recognized writer yet burdened by a writing block like "an ignoble version of the more or less noble renunciations of H.Roth, D. Fuchs, and J.Salinger." These divergent qualities are bound, he knows, by "something Waspish, theological, scared and insultingly ironical." As the American writer as Everyman, Bech - part joker, part victim - explores the postwar writer's inner crisis. [*Bech: A Book*, pp.9-10.]

complete his fourth, "long awaited," novel; a monstrous, fifteen year-long block has defeated him. The plot and the characters of "Think Big" elude him; the manuscript is a confusion of "hopeful beginnings," "a blasted dream." The novelist is embarrassed by this state of artistic silence, humiliated by the fact that the book has been mentioned in print for so many years that collectors write him "in some exasperation over their inability to procure a copy."[3] He is also perplexed to see himself drift away from "plain truth" and "further and further into treacherous realms of fantasy and, lately, of silence."[4] Upon receiving "the Melville Medal,"* "awarded every five years to that American author who has maintained the most meaningful silence," Bech's frustration is intensified.[5] Books, when one is no longer writing them, Bech realizes, uncannily continue to live, "to cast shuddering shadows toward the center of his life."[6] He feels besieged by layers of obscure guilt and confusion:

> Who was he? A Jew, a modern man, a writer, a bachelor, a loner, a loss. A con artist in the days of academic modernism undergoing a Victorian shudder. A white monkey hung far out on a spindly heaventree of stars. A fleck of dust condemned to know it is a fleck of dust. A mouse in a furnace. A smothered scream.[7]

He is both tormented and puzzled by the fact that his literary celebrity grows as his artistic power declines, that his readers extend a nearly inexhaustible grace period. He is "more and more hounded by homage," venerated by literary worshipers and honorary societies, invited to give lectures and attend symposia, to represent his country abroad.[8]

Bech's complaint is familiar. Struggling for fame while blocked is for writer-heroes a uniquely inter-locking phenomenon that often leads to long-lasting angst

---

*Harold Brodkey recently experienced this historical-literary irony. Upon publishing *The Runaway Soul* (1991), which had been "long-awaited", repeatedly announced, and highly-praised since the early sixties, *Time* magazine reviewed it under the title: "The 30-Year Writer's Block" [*Time*, November 25, 1991.]

mingled with farce. Preserving experience, making sense of it, become less important than retaining a thwarted dream, acting out an obsession, overcoming a sense of numbness.

Harry Lesser, the novelist in Bernard Malamud's *The Tenants*, is imprisoned by artistic obsession.* His suspended life and precarious sense of self depend on the success of the novel, which, after ten years' labor, he is unable to finish. In his twenties he published two novels, "the first good, the next bad." The good one earned him critical respect; the failure, made into a film, gave him merely "enough to live on." Success, Lesser realizes, is critical if a writer wants to be "thought of as an ongoing concern, not a freak who had published a good first novel and shot his wad."[9] The book, entitled "The Promised End," mirrors his own dilemma; he hopes that the process of writing will change him as a man, teach him to love "generously, fluently," in "a manner befitting an old ideal," give him an identity.[10] In the event, the writing turns into a self-made penitentiary. Like Malamud's earlier heroes Lesser is a schlemiel attempting to realize a literary vision which continues to evade him, a writer who, while searching for a new life, faces unexpected humiliations.

In *The Tenants*, another writer moves uninvited into the abandoned apartment building and proves to be a racial/aesthetic/political challenger. Willie Spearmint, an unpublished writer resembling Malcolm X (or Eldridge Cleaver) whose pseudonym - Bill Spear - is "part surname, part tribal hunting weapon, plus overtone of Shakespeare," plans to work on his first novel, a strongly race-conscious, largely autobiographical expression of the black anger of the 1960s.[11] Having no experience as a writer, he demands that Lesser read his manuscript for style, not message. When Lesser urges him to open up to the demands of a more elaborate form and artistic detachment, the black writer lashes back furiously. He fears that Lesser, a white man

---

*Malamud wrote several novels about artist-protagonists who are typically entrapped in a creative no exit. In "The Man in the Drawer" (1968), the writer Levitansky is trapped, literally and figuratively, in the totalitarian Soviet Union. In *Pictures of Fidelman* (1969), the painter hero is imprisoned in artistic perfectionism. William Dubin, in *Dubin's Lives*, a successful freelance biographer, is bound by the illusion that his biography on D.H. Lawrence will lend him a new life and activate his suppressed sexual and artistic vitality.

and a Jew, wants to distort his politically informed perception and message, which is a call for a Black revolution and the killing of whites. Tensions rise to the point of open hostilities. Each renders the other unable to write by destroying his manuscript or work place. Finally, as the novel closes, the two writers fight a duel set in a "grassy clearing in the bush," amid "moss-dripping, rope-entwined trees."[12] Feeling "the anguish of the other," they exchange deadly (and simultaneously symbolic) blows: Lesser smashes Spearmint's skull, Spearmint castrates Lesser.

The Tenants is a rich, many-layered parable about American writers in the 1960s. The white man's fiction, basically apolitical, concerns identity and the capacity to love, while the black man's work involves the felt need for struggle and revolution. Lesser lacks commitment to the Other; Spearmint's talent is drained by his rage and vengeance. Lesser argues the importance of distance and form, Spearmint views his writing as a catalyst for racial consciousness. Both try to improve on life through art while remaining victims of artistic deadlocks and racial/cultural stereotypes.

Twenty years after *The Tenants* Don DeLillo similarly couples a novelist's creative impasse and withdrawal to an unexpected confrontation with political issues. Bill Gray, in *Mao II* (1991), cannot proceed with his work in progress. He has spent years in seclusion, rewriting the same sentences repeatedly. The pressure to complete his novel ruins him - a worn-out hostage to literature, an alcoholic and a hypochondriac trapped in a prison house of "self-exaggeration."

> It's the self-important fool that keeps the writer going. I exaggerate the pain of writing, the pain of solitude, the failure, the rage, the confusion, the helplessness, the fear, the humiliation. The narrower the boundaries of my life, the more I exaggerate myself.[13]

Like Lesser, Bill yearns for success, yet he fears that by publishing he will destroy the romantic image of himself as a talented but reclusive author. Bill's assistant, Scott, tries to persuade the novelist to shelve the manuscript. Only by not publishing,

Scott argues, does the author's fame continue to grow. Bill knows the advantage of being famously unseen and uncreative in America; unpublished for some thirty years, he remains the country's leading literary icon. The corrupt "image world" in which we live, he figures, intrigues people who are also eager to "mock" and "dirty up" the famous. The less a writer is seen the more he is.

> In a mosque, no images. In our world we sleep and eat the image and pray to it and wear it too. The writer who won't show his face is encroaching on holy turf. He's playing God's own trick.[14]

Yet, in artistic terms, less is not more; Bill's celebrated withdrawal brings overwhelming suffering and loneliness. He is aware that his medium is weakened, that the writer's role is diminished by the white noise of television and news, by advertisements, gossip and countless distractions. The society has become indifferent to artists and writers.

Tired of modern times, of his self-imposed monastic existence, also of his controllers, Scott and Karen, Bill escapes to London, then to the Middle East, ostensibly to help a poet-hostage; but in truth to share, or incorporate, violence. In terrorism and hostage-taking he recognizes the power to shape sensibility and thought writers once had.

> He could have told George he was writing about the hostage to bring him back, to return a meaning that had been lost to the world....When you inflict punishment on someone who is not guilty...you begin to empty the world of meaning and erect a separate mental state...replacing real things with plots and fictions. One fiction taking the world narrowly into itself, the other fiction pushing out toward the social order, trying to unfold into it.[15]

DeLillo's *Mao II* expands an established theme in earlier writer-novels like Bellow's *Humboldt's Gift*, Irving's *The World According to Garp*, Mailer's *The Armies of the*

Night. That is, the American writer is both distracted (or deadlocked) and stimulated by social aberrations. Unable to ignore the state of the world, yet eager to protect his artistic sensibilities, he is increasingly ready to confront the sources of his torment. Doing so brings him to the existential brink of his integrity as a writer and his very being as a man.

Those novels that focus on the writer's inner conflicts portray a hero whose life is equally unquiet and distorted, affected by the laws of the market rather than the rigors of artistic motivation. Tony Lamont, in Sorrentino's *Mulligan Stew*, becomes increasingly paranoiac about his failure to achieve popularity and critical acclaim. His novel in progress eludes him, critics and publishers are dismissive. Deeply distressed, he constantly reassures himself and others that he is a talented and high-minded artist engaged in a serious project. In moments of doubt, however, he admits:

I really want to throw the whole thing away and compose a Gothic romance 'by Viola Tremble' - the moors sullen under lightning, the cold and eerie house, the howling dogs, the rain, the secret in the attic....

Then he adds:

What I mean is that I want to get out of this "career" that I have chosen. Or is it that I simply want financial success?[16]

Lamont's lonely and loveless life oscillates between the desire to wield the "moral" authority of the traditional novelist, and achieve the financial success of today's bestselling hack.[17] Yet having both worlds remains impossible because Lamont's artistic powers are diminished, while he himself becomes increasingly confused and hostile towards his audience. Jealous and aggressive, Lamont behaves like a desperate clown in search of applause. By projection, he describes a contemporary novelist's plight and, with heavy irony, bemoans the havoc of the contemporary writer's life:

> '...this faker of gladdening twists, collector of grist and of swill': 'He can
> write all right,' reviewers would say. Yet nor gleam nor ray of Yankee
> success lanced the dreary mess this writer made of his life.[18]

Bruce Gold, a writer and English professor in Joseph Heller's *Good as Gold*
(1979), experiences comparable anxiety concerning the Jewish experience in
America. "How can I write about the Jewish experience, when I don't even know
what it is?" he asks himself, then reflects: "I don't think I've ever run into an effective
anti-Semite."[19] Indeed, he knows very little of ethnic values. He regards his own
family as repulsive and irritating and perceives their smug, bourgeois, "close" life
as a lie and a bore. His father, a tyrant of "unpredictable wrath," reprimands him for
everything he is and does. His stepmother eagerly adds spite to hurt:

> 'I don't like you either....You admire money and you idolize the people who
> have it. You crave success. Wouldn't it be funny,' she went on, and cackled
> at him with a gleam of satanic wickedness in her eye, 'if he isn't even your
> real father and you've been taking all this criticism from him for nothing all
> these years? Wouldn't it be funny if you aren't even Jewish? You don't even
> know the language and the holidays, do you?'[20]

Gold is unhappy with his marriage, his writing and his teaching. Feeling lost
and diminished, he dreams of recognition, of power and money. What he is offered
instead is falsehood and humiliation. When a friend, who is a typically devious and
unscrupulous White House staff member, promises an influential government post,
Gold sees it as an attractive alternative to his dull life. For Gold, Henry Kissinger is
the embodiment of the Jewish manipulator who has shrewdly managed success in
the corridors of power. "How he loved and resented that hissing name."[21] But when
Gold looks closer at government bureaucracy, he is dismayed. He is deprived of his

privacy, crudely manipulated, and denied any opportunity to earn the public reputation he was promised. Filled with a terrible envy, consumed by guilt, unable to disengage himself from the degrading struggle for power and influence, he finally feels "distressed he might succeed."[22]

Although writer-heroes openly and compulsively document their failures and the resulting anguish, they rarely concede to utter paralysis or despair. Even Malamud's Lesser, one of the more monastic characters, pursues social engagements on occasion and conducts a torrid love-affair with his rival's girlfriend. In fact, they all express the hope at some point that their suffering is only temporary, and that one day their writing will be appreciated.

While awaiting success, these writer-heroes look for temporary self-assurance or satisfaction. Frequently, they find comfort in bizarre, risky, even criminal involvements. To garner at least "a discernible fraction of the *parnusseh* Kissinger was raking in from his own memoirs," Gold decides to present a thesis that would "excite attention"; he proclaims that Kissinger is not a Jew.

> ...he felt mutinously that he had as much right to falsehood, bias, and distortion in *his* memoirs of Kissinger as Kissinger did in his own memoirs of Kissinger and had exercised in public office.[23]

Similarly distraught, artistically unproductive and physically debilitated, thinking he "was *not* a sick man - he was *fighting* the idea of himself as sick," Zuckerman, in *The Anatomy Lesson*, becomes unexpectedly impatient, excessive, even violent. On the way to Chicago, where he wants to begin "a second life" studying medicine, he pretends to strangers that he is an unscrupulous New York porno king and a publisher of "Lickety Split," a hard-core publication.[24] Introducing himself to one nonplussed listener he uses the name of his adversary, the critic Milton Appel.

In *Music for Chameleons* (1980), Truman Capote recurringly focuses on the element of danger and violence in the contemporary writer's life. He quotes James's famous line from *The Middle Years*: "We live in the dark, we do what we can, the rest is the madness of art," only to stress the affinity of crime and writing.

> And the darkest part of the dark, the maddest part of madness, is the relentless gambling involved. Writers, at least those who take genuine risks, who are willing to bite the bullet and walk the plank, have a lot in common with another breed of lonely men - the guys who make a living shooting pool and dealing cards.[25]

In *Answered Prayers*, the writer persona, P.B. Jones, is a gambler and risk-taker. In his mid-thirties, he has published only one book, *Answered Prayers*, which was panned by the critics; even his own agent tells him: "professionalism is beyond you."[26] But Jones knows that the animosity is caused by his treachery and gross vulgarity, which are reflected in the novel. "I am a whore and always have been," he admits to himself. He writes of America's public figures* with unscrupulous derision and spite, fills his book with sexual scandal and vicious gossip.** He knows he deserves his readers' scorn:

> ...the prospect of going back to New York made my stomach lurch and dip with roller-coaster aggressiveness....It seemed to me I could never reenter that city, where I now had no friends and many enemies, unless preceded by marching bands and all the confetti of success.[27]

Admittedly, few heroes, or their creators, actively court the contempt of their

---

*Capote's own friends among them, some under their real names, or only thinly disguised.

**Capote's *Answered Prayers* contains similar material. Many readers, having recognized themselves in print, thereafter shunned Capote. In one case, the model for his murderess, Ann Hopkins, died of an overdose. "*Answered Prayers* is dismayingly vulgar: vulgar in humor...vulgar in style...," observes John Richardson, a critic and Capote's acquaintance. "The only prayers that interest the author are crassly materialistic and libidinous ones: unscrupulous hookers of either sex out to entrap rich husbands - that sort of thing." [John Richardson, A Côté Capote, *The New York Review of Books*, Dec. 17, 1987.]

audience. Most, including characters created by Kosinski, Heller, or Exley, strive to attain a balance, frequently with a cheerful disposition, between their fascination with, or proclivity for, the disruptive aspects of life and minimal decorum. They often pride themselves on living dangerously while remaining intact as moral agents and creative artists. The longing for spiritual contentment and social status, which was vital for earlier protagonists like Jack London's Martin Eden, is replaced by a desire to be nationally recognized, to write bestsellers, to achieve fame. The declared failure to get on with the work is all too often an oblique way of bemoaning the lack of success.

THE DEATH OF THE GARRET ARTIST

In the past, American writer-heroes assumed an idealistic stance toward their craft, ostentatiously scorning popularity and wealth. Novels featuring writers by Howells, James, Norris, London and Farrell, to cite a few notable examples, condemned writing for the market place and renounced celebrity - the perceived threat to artistic integrity. Some spoke contemptuously of those who catered to popular tastes. James held it as a solemn truth that writers who worshipped "the idols of the market" did so at the cost of their integrity and their art, and were likely to stray "the way dishonor lies."[28] Frank Norris saw the writer's independence as his greatest achievement. Like other naturalists, he believed in Zola's creed that the writer, being the priest of "the high lesson of reality," should not be influenced or sponsored.[29] More recently, James T. Farrell, though aware that a writer cannot control the social environment of literature and is often forced to become an artistic martyr, still claimed that whoever lets "a chance literary agent, a chance Hollywood producer, a chance publisher to violate his artistic honor with a fat contract," turns himself into "a wretched hack."[30] Sherwood Anderson thought that fame was actually detrimental to the artist. He once said: "Fame is no good, my dear. Take it away from me."[31] Hemingway frequently cautioned that money spells ruin. In

A Moveable Feast he tells Fitzgerald that remaking good stories into "salable magazine stories" is "whoring."[32] Fitzgerald is presented as a supreme example of an author who was corrupted by writing hastily and with profit in mind.

Fitzgerald was obviously not the first writer to succumb to the market place. Poe often wrote quickly and badly while serving as editor of commercial literary journals aimed at the common reader and quick profit. Twain lived extravagantly and gladly gave public lectures, in part, to enhance his prestige as a writer and to ensure market success. Like his hero, Martin Eden, who decides to abandon ambition and "move to Grub Street," Jack London wrote trash in order to live in luxury on exorbitant royalties.[33]

But these writers' commercialism has always been seen as an unfortunate exception to the noble rule. The pseudo-romantic image of the artist who resists fame and wealth remained the ethical paradigm for more than one hundred and fifty years, and was widely accepted well into the 1950s. Portraits of young literary monks, scornful of society's ideals of success and acquisition, populate the novels of Henry Miller and Burroughs, Holmes and Kerouac, early Bellow and Mailer. Characteristically, these writers live in shabby garrets or rented rooms, content themselves with very little, see themselves as outsiders on the frontier surrounded by bourgeois mediocrity and bureaucratic intimidation. "The misunderstood genius working obscurely in the garret was the role model," muses Ronald Sukenick reminiscing about his own early efforts to enter the world of serious literary life. In *Up*, he presents himself as a novice writer who is disturbed more by the perplexities of the postwar psyche, or the fatuous pretensions of modernism, than by the rats. But in the mid-eighties Sukenick takes an ironic view of his earlier pose. He concedes that "the truth is that in this country the myth of the genius in the garret was always a middle class soap opera."[34]

By the late 1950s and throughout the 1960s the mystique of the garret and the underground begins to crumble. The rules of production and the laws of the capitalist market place inevitably affect the hitherto relatively isolated and independent lifestyle of the American writer. His status changes. It shifts, as one critic put it, "from that of an independent creator to that of a wage earner."[35] Universities hire authors as professors and government grants are available to promising writers, even to young avant-garde rebels. In the mid-fifties, *Time* magazine observes that garret artists are "not much in evidence" because "most writers like to live like people and if they must be in attics, they want them air-conditioned."[36] The vocation of writing ceases to be associated with poverty and becomes a desirable, profitable and therefore attractive profession.

During the sixties, a period of political liberation and sexual revolution giving rise to new levels of social and cultural tolerance, writers felt that many older assumptions about art had become outdated. Effectively, they abandoned their mission to oppose and discredit the establishment, leaving the field to hippies and counterculture cults of all descriptions. "The modernist cult of failure," Sukenick observes, "collides with the middle-class cult of success....Subterraneans wanted simultaneously to rant at Moloch and be part of Moloch, as if you could bite the hand of oppression and then demand it feed you."

> The ideas of European modernism were losing their grip on a new generation of consciously American artists to whom they no longer seemed appropriate. The academy and then government began opening their arms to the dissenting intelligentsia, and one began to hear talk of successful intellectuals, formerly a contradiction in terms.[37]

Norman Podhoretz's autobiographical *Making It* (1967)[*] renounces the cult of the garret and spreads the new gospel of literary success. Podhoretz, a successful Jewish critic, writer and editor, admits that, although he was brought up to believe that "the serious life of the mind" meant "inevitably a life of relative deprivation," because being successful meant being corrupt, he discovered, while in his thirties, that it was "better to be a success than a failure," that money and power were

---

[*] Like Seymour Krim's essay under the same title, though with an exclamation mark.

"important" and "desirable," and that fame was "unqualifiedly delicious."[38] American intellectuals are caught up in an unresolved contradiction, Podhoretz further explains: they are fascinated with fame and success, but are not prepared to talk honestly about them. They were told that "success was supreme, even the only, American value"; yet, as sex had been "the dirty little secret" of Victorian times, so success continues to be the guilty secret of the American writer's life.[39]

> On the one hand, "the exclusive worship of the bitch-goddess SUCCESS," as William James put it in a famous remark, "is our national disease"; on the other hand, a contempt for success is the consensus of the national literature for the past hundred years or more.[40]

For Podhoretz the only American writer "capable of perfect honesty on the subject of success" in the 1960s is Norman Mailer, the novelist who was not taken seriously because he produced a bestselling novel at a time when market success was still considered antithetical to literary respect.[41]

Mailer was, in fact, guilty of other, similarly "inadmissable violations." In *Advertisements for Myself* he confessed he was dissatisfied with the fact that the reading public did not bestow on him the measure of popularity it accorded Hemingway, Faulkner or Steinbeck. Being "just one of the big men in town" was seen as "tiring, much too tiring" for him. He also admits that, having succeeded with his first novel, *The Naked and the Dead*, he wanted to prove he could turn out another bestseller and thus be "the first serious writer of my generation to have a bestseller twice." Claiming two bestselling novels would render him invulnerable to criticism, because, Mailer explained, "the literary world suffers a spot of the national taint - a serious writer is certain to be considered major if he is also a bestseller; in fact, most readers are never convinced of his value until his books do well."[42]

When Mailer fails to sustain market approval through his fifties novels, he expresses frustration, aggression and hostility in his writing and in his own life. Criticized, he assumes the role of an outlaw, a warrior and a revolutionary involved in political campaigns, brushes with the law, conflicts with his wives, confrontations with feminists and homosexuals, provocative articles in *Esquire* magazine, pugnacious interviews.

In *The Armies of the Night*, published a year after *Making It*, Mailer couches his hunger for success in a brave new idiom. He presents himself as an outsized figure: excessive, vulgar, schizoid, a clownish and shameless celebrity whose crises reflect the painful and comic confusion of the contemporary American writer, but also serve his obsessive search for self-promotion. Calling himself "the best writer in America" and "a snob of the worst sort," he balances precariously on the verge of buffoonery and self-mockery - a one-man publicity show which is simultaneously brilliant and absurd.[43] His sense of irony and humor undercuts his role as the ridiculous debauched literary personage; indeed, his defects can be regarded as endearing traits.

Mailer's personal bravura, the compulsion to confront America directly, as Mailer the writer, to deal with his experience on his own terms, to mingle intellect with public exposure, to treat writing as a stage for personal exploits and commentaries, begins a tendency that permeates the American novel in the 1970s and 1980s. Examples abound: Barth, Vonnegut, Roth, Kesey, Exley, Theroux, Capote, Kosinski, who appear as characters in fiction under their real, or only slightly disguised names, or Bellow, Malamud, Updike, or Irving, who create fictional alter egos, toy with the themes of popularity and power, with glamour and media hype - along with the complications and frustrations of fame and its vicissitudes. Though most of these authors prefer their exposures, or confessions, or brushes with America, to be playful and evasive rather than curt and direct, they, like Mailer, usually desire not only critical and financial success, but sustained popularity and cultural influence.

Yet to attain celebrity writers endure rituals they often detest: they are expected to act as celebrities, performers, entertainers, they are interviewed, obliged to take part in talk-shows and to go on publicity tours. This widely-practiced, media-enhanced pageantry is, Leo Braudy, the author of *The Frenzy and Renown: Fame and Its History* (1986) points out, an indispensable element of the firmly-rooted, highly ritualistic system of America's "publicity culture," a phenomenon that transcends the secular-materialistic mode:

> Fame is really our religion in America. And we have a constantly changing calendar of saints whom we encounter in our media churches, especially films and television, which have the largest congregations.[44]

A scene in Kosinski's *The Hermit of 69th Street* illustrates well Braudy's view. Norbert Kosky sees the presentation of the Oscars in which he is asked to announce the winners as an enormous religious ceremony, "the Grand Mass" of Hollywood. High-strung, risking a heart-attack, bullied by the arrogant figures of the tv "sacristy," he, "our literary Ministrant," "our altar boy," opens the nomination address with "The Bible tells us that in the beginning was the word."[45] Such exposure of the writer, or the artist, is to him painfully grotesque. Drawn into this comedy of art as excess, Kosky goes through the nightmare ordeal, masquerades as a super star, makes a fool of himself. Yet Kosky knows that old definitions of artistic restraint and dignity are no longer useful, that today's writer is faced with an overwhelming, culturally sanctified, market-shaped mentality, which he has to accept fully to avoid isolation and neglect.

Though Mailer and Kosinski approach the writer's struggle with the literary market differently - Mailer claims the writer has to adhere to its rules, Kosinski's Kosky realizes he cannot escape them - both accept that the man-of-letters can no longer ignore the prevailing consumer ethos. Other prominent authors share these sentiments. Saul Bellow (who, unlike Mailer or Kosinski avoids publicity) acknowledges that "It's all or nothing in the U.S., and if you don't make the celebrity circuit you are wretchedly ignored."[46] Susan Sontag sees the impact of the market as a potentially dangerous factor:

> The temptations of egotism and of commercialism are such that you have to

be very eccentric to be a good writer in this country, to love literature above all and not be mainly concerned with self-promotion.[47]

W.H. Auden made a similar observation in the late 1940s. He predicted that the surge of postwar materialism would alter American writers' attitudes to art. It will be increasingly difficult, he said, for the writer "to resist the temptations to cheapen his product" because he not only "suffers from a lack of popular success," but, having grown up in a society "where the business *ethos* is dominant," he finds it hard "not to believe that art is...a commodity like a motor car whose sales and profits are an accurate indication of value."[48]

Auden's prediction proved accurate. The postwar era brought vast changes in the production and distribution of books. The paperback, mass produced, widely circulated and advertized - a powerful medium in itself - has indeed become a cheap commodity for the mass audience: a glossy, spiritual quick fix. Meanwhile, the writer, owing to public exposure on nationwide talk shows, evolves an image: his personality, his private life, his statements supplement the printed work and amplify the dimensions of textual meaning. "The American writer, if he is not careful...may end up eminent and bad, thinking of his reader as a customer, as a consumer of a product, tested and true, of which he is the producer," observers a critic in the late 1980s.[49]

One may be tempted to argue that the champions of artistic purity were idealistic by default; after all the writer in the past did not deal with massive technology and media-enhanced wealth and power. Leslie Fiedler goes farther. He believes that the defenders of the purity of literary craft were merely hypocrites who publicly despised and secretly envied the lure of wealth. He argues that we are confronted with yet another literary myth, "as strong and pertinacious as any myth by which we live," the myth that the writer in America has written for art, not for money. "Our eminent writers," Fiedler states, "have not typically spoken with equal candor on the subject of literature and lucre." Their affected idealism and lack of honesty are responsible for the fact that "there is no respectable American book which portrays sympathetically an author who made good" before the middle of the 20th century.[50]

THE DISTRESS OF SUCCESS

While Fiedler is making these observations in the early 1980s, novelists are already re-examining the American writer's relationship to money and fame. As a case in point, Bellow's Charlie Citrine, the eminently successful author in *Humboldt's Gift*, sees his sudden wealth as a welcome cultural vagary: "such sums as I made, made themselves. Capitalism made them for dark comical reasons of its own."[51] He is proud of his silver Mercedes, his valuable Persian carpets, his exclusive club where he plays squash. He enjoys being dominated by an attractive, but materialistic mistress, Renata.

Yet success comes at a price. He remembers that Von Humboldt Fleisher, his erstwhile celebrated friend and spiritual inspiration, made malicious comments on Citrine's sudden affluence, that he drew money from Citrine's account to buy a car. Citrine worries that his ex-wife sues him to secure exorbitant alimony in order to ruin him, that his lawyers and a business partner swindle him, that IRS agents are "after" him. He is harassed, threatened and humiliated by a cheap thug who destroys his car and later offers to become his business partner. Citrine remembers that Humboldt, though forgotten and impoverished in the 1950s, was, in better times, familiar with fame and wealth. Humboldt aspired to be a "divine artist, a man of visionary states and enchantments, Platonic possession"; he also wanted to be rich and famous. Money meant freedom to him; patterns of success, "passionately lived out," provided a sense of liberation. "What kind of American would I be," Humboldt would say, "if I were innocent about money?"[52] He both fought and celebrated the superiority of the material over the spiritual. He instructed Citrine on the need to "get around pragmatic America," hoped that a blending of the poet's imagination and America's money-oriented rationalism would help free and improve the society.

Refused the role of an artist-capitalist, he "spilled dirt, spread scandal, and uttered powerful metaphors." Upon reflection, Citrine decides that Humboldt told his "hungry for culture" and "curious about genius" readers what they expected to hear, the "tale" of the artist's "unhappiness and persecution."[53]

Several years after Humboldt's death, at the time when the "agony is too deep, the disorder too big for art enterprises undertaken in the old way," Citrine wonders if art's relationship with life can be revised.[54] He yearns to wield the kind of creative power and influence Humboldt assumed for himself. He also wishes to maintain the success he has enjoyed at the time Humboldt had already lost it.

> It was my turn to be famous and to make money, to get heavy mail, to be recognized by influential people, to be dined at Sardi's and propositioned in padded booths by women who sprayed themselves with musk, to buy Sea Island cotton underpants and leather luggage, to live through the intolerable excitement of vindication. (I was right all along!) I experienced the high voltage of publicity. It was like picking up a dangerous wire fatal to ordinary folk. It was like rattlesnakes handled by hillbillies in a state of religious exaltation.[55]

Citrine is aware that Humboldt was flawed in both his reasoning and his behavior, that he was unable to reconcile his uncouth American mentality with often contradictory views of the function of the poet, along with an inability to adjust to the times.

> Humboldt wanted to drape the world in radiance, but he didn't have enough material. His attempt ended at the belly. Below hung the shaggy nudity we know so well...the radiance he dealt in was the old radiance and it was in short supply.[56]

But he is also convinced that his deceased friend is an example of an artist who nourishes and gratifies the public through failure. Failed poets are loved by Americans, "but loved because they just can't make it here."

> The country is proud of its dead poets. It takes terrific satisfaction in the poets' testimony that the USA is too tough, too big, too much, too rugged, that American reality is overpowering. And to be a poet is a school thing, a skirt thing, a church thing. The weakness of the spiritual powers is proved in the childishness, madness, drunkenness, and despair of these martyrs.[57]

Like Fiedler, Citrine feels readers judge artists by false standards. Those who have not resisted the bitch goddess are usually seen as victims of debased American values, rather than those who wanted to succeed but failed. Citrine hopes he can avoid Humboldt's fate and escape the traps of alienation and paranoia. He ponders about the need of a new balance between art and power, and about a new relationship between writer and reader. "What we needed was a new radiance altogether," he muses.[58] When Citrine learns that Humboldt had willed him a legacy, "Humboldt's gift," in the form of valuable scenarios, he feels that Humboldt had suffered and died for him, also for the whole new generation of writers who aspire to handle their profession without the former naive straightforwardness and idealism about their aims - and without the fear of fame.

Throughout the 1970s and 1980s, a number of novels link the writer's fascination with success to similarly fragile spiritual allegiances and uneasy material dependencies. "I wanted the wealth and the power that fame would bring," admits Frederick Exley, the narrator of Frederick Exley's *A Fan's Notes* (1968). Vague about the rules of good writing, he is certain that he must produce "The Big Book."[59] Truman Capote serves as a model of success. "I knew that like me," Exley reminisces, "he was young, and that, as I hoped to be, he was famous."[60] When success eludes him, Exley identifies with Frank Gifford, star athlete of the Giants football team. But Gifford's achievement is too distant, inimitable. Exley's dreams of glory collapse and so does his life. He drinks heavily, loses his job, commits himself to a mental institution. When he learns that the critic and writer, Edmund Wilson, owns a house a few miles from his home, his "literary" fantasies come alive. He reads and re-reads Wilson, fantasizes about having a "literary duologe" (sic) with him, of doing "something absolutely Wilsonian."[61] When he realizes he will not be another Wilson, Exley, like many before him, consigns his manuscript to the flames.

In *Pages from a Cold Island* (1975), the Exley persona's search for inner order is again linked to the dream of financial-literary success. Royalties from *A Fan's Notes* do not quite allow for "payments on a Mark IV Continental."[62] When he learns that his Wilson has died, he becomes obsessed with the celebrated critic's writing career. Clearly, though not explicitly, Exley-as-hero is fascinated by Wilson's discipline and craftsmanship, qualities that do not prevail in his own indisciplined, drunken, and periodically suicidal life.

In *Last Notes from Home* (1988), the third novel in the series, the Exley persona continues the sad, also desperately humorous, tale of a novelist like himself who, while trying to capture a sense of identity and sanity, clings to the myth of American glory and success. Failing this, he finds himself, as *A Fan's Notes* concludes, "running: obsessively *running*."[63]

Knowing he cannot be "up to Norman Mailer," the ambitious but unrecognized poet/novelist in Max Apple's "Inside Norman Mailer" (*The Oranging of America*, 1976), imagines himself defeating his idol in a boxing match. "Why envy from afar when I can pummel you in a lighted ring." The fighting, however, is literary-ideological rather than physical.

> The bell has moved us into a new field of force. We drop our pens. The spotlight is the glare of eternity, and what it has all come to is simply the matter of Truth. "Existentialist" I call him...."Dated existentialist. Insincere existentialist. Jewish existentialist...." I hit him with this smooth combination, but he continues to rush me bearlike, serene, full of skill and power.

Unexpectedly, the narrator not only survives the first round, but lands a right that leaves Mailer "dazed and hurt." He sees fear in Mailer's eyes and "the beast in his soul." But he wants more: the quintessence of the novelist's fame.

> Yes, I can wait, Norm, until you come to me in mid-ring with all that bulk and experience. Come to me with your strength, your wisdom, your compassion, and your insight.[64]

The young Nathan Zuckerman, an emerging writer of only four published stories in Philip Roth's *The Ghost Writer*, must choose between someone like the ascetic and reclusive, recently "discovered" writer of Russian-Jewish background, E.I. Lonoff, and the successful, rich and self-publicized author, Felix Abravanel.[*] Visiting Lonoff at home gives Zuckerman an opportunity to compare the man's severe style and restrained attitudes with the dashing manners of Abravanel, whom he had met earlier. Zuckerman admires Lonoff's asceticism and self-control, but is appalled by the monotonous rigor of his life, "a man, his destiny, and his work - all one. What a terrible triumph!"[65] He recognizes that the reclusive and austere writer deprives himself of worldly experience, human contact, sense of manhood and a rich emotional life. At the same time he fears that celebrity means aspiring for public image and power, betraying one's ideals, exposing and complicating everyone's life, his own included.

Zuckerman knows that either lifestyle is inevitably linked to deeper and more tangled commitments. He wants to embrace the vastness and energy of life, to be a part of the unrestrained world of love and sex, to be freed of responsibility toward his orthodoxically-minded family and Jewish readers. When he meets Amy, an attractive and mysterious young woman, a former student of Lonoff and now possibly his mistress, he thinks of having sex with her, imagines her as Anne Frank,

---

[*]Abravanel is usually recognized in criticism as a composite of Bellow and Mailer; Lonoff is compared to Malamud and Singer.

visualizes himself marrying her: an indication that he would like to be an artist who combines spontaneous imagination with a zest for sensuality.

In *Zuckerman Unbound* (1981), the novelist is a middle-aged and successful author of four novels. He now embraces the world he once rejected as an idealistic young writer. His recent book, the bestselling shocker "Carnovsky," has earned him a million dollars, fame and luxury. Yet Zuckerman is unable to deal adequately with the confusion of success. "All this, this luck - what did it mean? Coming so suddenly, and on such a scale, it was as baffling as a misfortune," muses the novelist on his way to discuss with an investment specialist how to secure his massive royalties.[66] A stranger recognizes him on the bus and asks what he, "with your dough," is doing there. Others accost him in the street, send him fan or hate mail, take him for his lascivious hero Carnovsky, offer sex, jokes and insults.[67] Tabloids publish stories about his daily actions. Someone threatens to kidnap his mother. Zuckerman's life becomes increasingly unreal and out of control. He is now the object of the society's literature-enhanced writer fantasy, as well as the victim of much unexpected cruelty. He sees himself, the title suggests, as a latter-day Prometheus who has given mankind the gift of his book - which was to free civilization of the darkness of sexual repression and prejudice. Yet, he remains misunderstood, victimized and abused, "bound to the cross of your own cruelfiction!" as Joyce expressed it in *Finnegans Wake*.[68]

No one sympathizes with Zuckerman, now the victim of his own success. His friend and literary agent says he has never seen anyone "make such a fiasco of fame and fortune." He is scornful of Zuckerman's former literary idealism and unassuming lifestyle: "I know about all those index cards you carry around in your wallet: fortifying quotations from the great literary snobs about fame giving satisfaction only to mediocre vanities." He would like to see the writer enjoy his worldly accomplishment: employ a household staff, live sumptuously, embrace his popularity.[69] He puts Zuckerman's literary triumph in the broader perspective of contemporary American cynicism:

But if you recall, Nathan dear, being really you was what was driving you crazy only a few short years ago. You told me so yourself. You felt stultified writing "proper, responsible" novels....Well, you have successfully conducted your novelistic experiment and now you are famous all over the haywire country for being highly haywire yourself, and you're even more stultified than before....You set out to sabotage your own moralizing nature, you set out to humiliate all your dignified, high-minded gravity, and now that you've done it, and done it with a relish of a real saboteur, now you're humiliated, you idiot, because nobody aside from you seems to see it as a profoundly moral and high-minded act![70]

The novel's motto (attributed to Lonoff, the disciplined author in *The Ghost Writer*) suggests that such assaults on Zuckerman were predictable:

Let Nathan see what it is to be lifted from obscurity. Let him not come hammering at our door to tell us that he wasn't warned.[71]

Zuckerman's complaints echo Citrine's: a writer's success, if it comes, is distressing because the society does not treat him with respect or in a realistic manner. He is all too often faced with his readers' perverse and implacable fantasies rooted in their inability to distinguish between the life of the author and his work, between "the illusionist and the illusion."[72]

Philip Roth has devoted several novels to this theme. In *The Anatomy Lesson* (1983) Zuckerman is tired of the paradoxes of popularity and the preposterous interpretations contrived by readers and critics. Additionally, he suffers from chronic excruciating pain in the neck, arms and shoulders which, his psychoanalyst insists, is a "self-inflicted" condition, a penance for "Carnovsky," the novel which contains "the tastelessness that had affronted millions and the shamelessness that had enraged his tribe."[73] Ready to see himself as the betrayer of his art, a failed artist forever chained to literary narcissism - "self-consciousness...to retrospection, to my dwarf drama" - he decides to give up writing.[74] His fame is repugnant to him - "It wasn't literary fame, it was sexual fame" - and so is the money, "a lot of money" that brings "a lot of embarrassment."[75] He feels that by enrolling in medical school he will have a chance to deal with life's authentic narratives, stories that are definite and useful, and which have "a clear and practical purpose; *cure me*."[76] An accident (or a self-inflicted injury) puts him in a hospital, where, as the novel closes, he inspects the wounded and the sick, a healer trying to be useful; his "fanatical devotion" no longer wasted by "sitting with a typewriter alone in a room!"[77] *

When the writer happens to be Jewish, Roth asserts, popularity and success guarantee yet another backlash: the anger of his family, his friends, his community. In *The Ghost Writer* the youthful novelist realizes that his desire to write honestly about his life in Newark produces accusations of anti-Semitism. In *Zuckerman Unbound* the Jewish community is stirred and offended by the contents of Nathan's raunchy bestseller. He is accused of "depicting Jews in a peep-show atmosphere of total perversion."[78] His family, deeply ashamed, wishes their famous son made his fortune in some other way. His father calls him "bastard" on his deathbed. In *The Anatomy Lesson* the influential Jewish critic, Milton Appel, condemns Zuckerman for depicting "Jewish lives for the sake of belittling them" and sees him as "a sell-out to the pop-porno culture."[79] The novelist realizes that to be free as an artist he has to disengage himself from much of his own background. Yet the various attempts to do so are never fully successful.**

---

*Roth does not abandon here the theme of the writer's self-defeating reaction to success. In *The Counterlife*, Zuckerman reappears as a novelist of solid artistic confidence. He discovers that success, much like fiction-writing, goes well with hiding, masks and camouflaging, just as mixing facts and fiction, deftly and imaginatively, are effective evasive techniques. In *Deception, The Facts, Patrimony* and *Operation Shylock*, Zuckerman's confrontations with success are further examined by figures calling themselves Philip or Philip Roth.

**To Chaim Potok, a number of today's Jewish literary characters, including those in the novels of Roth, experience only a "periphery-to-periphery culture confrontation," and, like the authors who create them, are, "alienated, bewildered, contentious individuals, belonging nowhere, tenuously connected to culture and community, many committed only to the hermeneutics of doubt...." A Jewish writer, Potok believes, may feel like a multiple transgressor; he violates his background culture when he decides to adopt American values and when he decides to be a writer, but, perhaps most of all, when he realizes that being a writer in America means being a literary entertainer, being

Success, when it finally comes, surprises Updike's Henry Bech (*Bech is Back*). Prodded by his new wife, a woman of suburban and domestic sensitivity, he finishes writing the "ghastly tangle" of his novel "Think Big" and becomes a bestselling author with a million dollars in his account. *Vogue* announces that Bech is "in" again. "Bech Is Back" serves as the publisher's advertising slogan. Reviewers stress that the novel was "Fifteen Years in the Making." Reintroduced to the bright pop-cultural menu of America, Bech is interviewed, photographed, invited to exclusive parties, lionized at home and abroad.

Think Big in its shiny aqua jacket joined the Popsicles and roller coasters, baseball games and beach picnics as one of that summer's larky things....[80]

Bech sees his success as a spin-off of the absurd and vulgar but also comical spectacle of American marketing practices. He is ready to endure the accompanying inconveniences - including a surge of critical bitterness. Alfred Kazin calls "Think Big" "the squalid book we all deserve," Gore Vidal is surprised that it is "not quite as *vieux chapeau* as I had every reason to fear." *Time* laconically admits in a belated review that "Bech surprises."[81] No newcomer to literary success, Bech knows that the publicity he receives is not an appreciation of talent or insight, but the consequence of the massive whimsical forces that sanction commercialism. He is grateful, but not fooled. Deep inside he remains uneasy, vulnerable, constantly reminded that triumph demands as much as it gives.

The world, by one of those economic balancings whereby it steers, had at the same time given him success and taken from him the writer's chief asset, his privacy.[82]

---

insincere. "I didn't want to be an entertainment writer," Potok insists; "My religious world led me to a more sober view of the writing enterprise. I would not use words as slavish messengers of comfort and ease, but to explore seriously - I knew not what at that time in my life." [Chaim Potok, "The Invisible Map of Meaning: A Writer's Confrontations," *TriQuarterly*, Northwestern University, Spring/Summer, 1992, p.25.]

Then, an even more dismaying realization dawns on him: he now will be expected to write another novel. In point of fact, he has no choice.

Isadora Wing, the writer featured in Erica Jong's novels, admits, in *How to Save Your Own Life*, that she had always "lusted after fame, notoriety, adulation." To be a published writer is like being a "demigod," someone "blessed with a constant supply of love and self-assurance." Yet after establishing herself as a bestselling novelist, she discovers "the other side of the sun-house mirror of fame." Her life becomes "some sort of nightmare," a deception of multiple distortions:

> It was as if I had entered a room which very few are allowed to enter and which everyone on the outside believes to be incredibly beautiful, opulent, and magical. Once inside, you discover it is a hall of mirrors and all you see are myriad distortions of self, self, self.[83]

Like her male counterparts, Isadora blames the critics and the reading public for distorting and perverting everything she writes. She sees herself as "a fish gasping on the bed," tormented by merciless reviewers, "the fishermen reeling me in from the ceiling....They had me on the hook of my own mortality; fame was the bait I had swallowed and now it was stuck in my throat, stopping my screams."[84]

The readers, meanwhile, driven by envy and ambition, deluded by the glamor of the writer's existence, dream of grabbing a share. They "project their fantasies and frustrations on you," identify with the author's life, want to take it over. Isadora attempts to deal with the trauma of success and "visibility." She tells herself that she cannot be "plunged into despair, terror, fear of falling," that the only way "to transcend ambition" was "to go *through* the fame crazies":

> Only after that could I dedicate myself to what really mattered - to loving someone wholeheartedly, to working at my writing instead of going up in smoke as a media personality, to *using* success instead of letting it use me....

In spite of such resolutions, Isadora does not finally manage to merge her market success with personal fulfillment. She becomes "desperate" when she realizes how much she "had signed away, and how binding it was."[85] She concedes that however successful a woman artist may be, she is always suspended between a desire to shatter people's preconceptions of womanhood and a need to serve men, to remain feminine. Expressing such feelings, she betrays much anxiety, self-doubt and guilt which, mixed with a sense of dependence and masochism, lead to what male writers experience: intermittent urges to renounce artistic triumph, to retreat to an existence far from the allure of writing and publishing.

THE MENACING IMAGINATION

Nabokov, a talent cultivated on cross-cultural inspirations, demonstrates how stories of literary success, even in the world of mass uniformity and conformity, can be a matter of fanciful and dynamic developments. The protagonist of *Look at the Harlequins!*, for example, a distinguished Anglo-Russian novelist settled in the United States where he achieves financial success, deplores the loss of his youthful dreams of literary fame. He had hoped to be "a famous and free author, living in a free, universally respected Russia...on one of my splendid estates in the country...[a] great Russian writer"; but is instead saddled with a life of an émigré obsessed with the demonic and self-destructive urge to impersonate a shadowy nemesis, "that other writer who was and would always be incomparably greater, healthier, and crueler than your obedient servant." Elements of the historical, the political and the personal enveloped in mists of poetry and nostalgia combine with the delusional, the inane, the schizoid, the patently fantastic.[86]

American tales of literary success gone wrong are equally urgent, but characteristically less extensive and imaginative. In fact, they are often surprisingly bitter, even gruesome. They focus on the magnetic attraction the novelist's fame holds for assorted maniacs, perverts and criminals who, having learned that writing fiction today entails power and glamor, demand a share. Writer-heroes report that once they become celebrities they are accosted by people who try to exploit, intimidate, or ridicule - even destroy them, that they are exposed to a strange mixture of the worshipful, the profane and the villainous. Being implicated in this dark and dangerous side of popularity becomes, by the 1970s, more central and more conscience-shaping for protagonists than complaints concerning stalled writing or ungrateful readers.

Isadora Wing, in Jong's *Fear of Flying*, is warned that as a writer she will become "a fetish for all kinds of frustrated types." This indeed takes place. She receives "bizarre calls" from men expecting sexual adventures like those she describes in her novels. She feels like "public property...a whore."[87] Citrine, in *Humboldt's Gift*, often wonders why crime and culture, gangsterism and literary respectability mingle in the United States and invade the writer's privacy and stability. Rinaldo Cantabile, a man of raw aggression and "an agent of destruction," repeatedly humiliates him, vandalizes his Mercedes, offers to kill his wife, then coolly offers his services as the writer's procurer and business partner. Devlin Deboree, Ken Kesey's persona in *Demon Box*, worries about former and new followers visiting him on his farm in Oregon, to which he withdraws after the dissolution of the Merry Pranksters. Some of these visitors are dangerous criminals. Exley, the writer in *Last Notes from Home* (1988), is taken hostage by a deranged man, supposedly linked to the IRA and involved in arms deals. Kindled by espionage novels, he demands that Exley use him as a character in a book. The novelist in DeLillo's *Mao II* remembers brooding about death, imagining himself being killed "Not (by) a thief or deer hunter or holiday sniper but some dedicated reader."[88] He also recalls receiving, with no clue to its significance, a human finger in the mail. Norbert Kosky in Kosinski's *The Hermit of 69th Street* is badgered by various cranks who recognize him in his New York City milieu - including a bartender who is writing a dissertation on Kosky. He requests Kosky's private notes and interviews, suggests that the novelist reveal his erotic experiences. He is convinced that Kosky's reputation among gossip communists will make his research profitable and improve his social standing.

Garp and his mother, in *The World According to Garp*, learn early that the world's insanity and fanaticism reach writers via their readers. Jenny Field's autobiography not only establishes her as an outspoken feminist writer in America, but also exposes her to vicious fanatics. Eventually, she is shot dead at a rally by a man who blames her for the feminist movement. Garp is also eventually killed by crazed zealots infuriated by what he has written. He discovers that responding, in all sincerity and respect, to "hate mail" inspires an even more furious and aggressive response. A woman who consistently calls him "shithead" writes that her husband will "beat your brains to a pulp" if he writes her again.[89]

Roth's Zuckerman, after achieving fame (in *Zuckerman Unbound*), realizes that the price of a writer's success today includes being implicated in the world of perverts and blackmailers. A paranoid admirer, an ex-Marine called Alvin Pepler, who claims to be a writer himself, stalks Zuckerman, confesses "Carnovsky" is for him the kind of vision of life he has failed to live out. *"The man is mad,"* Zuckerman assumes, *"and fixed on me. Who is he behind those dark glasses? Me! He thinks he's me!"*[90] When the novelist refuses to meet his demands, the stalker becomes increasingly hostile. Zuckerman suspects that Pepler is linked to the well-read caller who demands fifty thousand dollars for not kidnapping the writer's mother. The man is sufficiently informed to refer to Zuckerman's controversial treatment of Jewish themes:

> Have a heart Zuck. Haven't you given her enough misery with that book? Don't make it any worse than it already is. Don't make it so that she regrets the day you were born, sonny.[91]

Appalled by this unexpected invasion from "life," Zuckerman secludes himself in his apartment, hires an answering service, and finally rents a limousine with an armed driver. He wonders how much of the murky unreality around him is inspired by his own imagination. Will he "beget still other Peplers conjuring up novels out of his -

novels disguising themselves as actuality itself, as nothing less than real?"[92]

The theme is developed in *The Counterlife*. Another crank admirer, having found Zuckerman in Jerusalem, demands that the novelist assists him in a hijacking of a plane on the return flight in order to force the Israelis to close the Yad Vashem museum. To him writers like Zuckerman infuse people with aberrant ideas:

All I know about cracking offensive jokes I learned at your great feet....You're a real father to me, Nathan. And not only to me - to a whole generation of pathetic fuck-ups. We're satirists *because* of you.[93]

In *Operation Shylock* a famous writer called Roth discovers that a man propagating radical views - the people of Israel should be lead out of the country and dispersed throughout Europe - has usurped his identity. When the infuriated yet fascinated "real" Roth travels to Jerusalem and attempts to track down the imposter, his life becomes a tangle of bizarre coincidences, conspiracies and covert intrigues. He is sucked into a labyrinthine plot which fuses fact and fiction, mingles the concepts of identity and fanaticism, and questions everyday reality.

In Gordon Lish's *Dear Mr. Capote* (1983), David, a criminal morbidly fascinated with Truman Capote, offers the famous novelist a profitable arrangement: exclusive rights to the story of his gruesome obsession - to kill forty-seven women, one for each year of his life. In order to earn "millions" Capote must "play his cards right."[94] Norman Mailer did not do so. Approached by David, "the nervy s.o.b. played himself right out of the picture....what he did is took me for a fool."[95] The killer, who claims he is a former radio announcer and a bank officer, explains how important it is for him to be "a famous celebrity," a "household word," in the papers and "on all of the channels."[96] Massive publicity, he imagines, will not only make him equal to successful writers like Capote or Mailer, but establish him as a permanent super-media figure. "Tonight, for example. In other words, 'Newsline' comes on. So what's her top story, your latest bestseller or Paki's (the name of his murderous knife) latest you know what?"[97]

Attuned to the times, David instructs Capote that his once famous account of two cold-blooded killers is no longer likely to shock the reader.

Hey, let's face it, I don't envy you having to write bestsellers for the kind of people you have today! The people of today wouldn't let you get to first base with something sleepy and nice. You take the great American classics like the ones you always write. They don't mean a thing to the caliber of people in this day and age! Believe me, these individuals, they're not laying out good money for one Kansas family all inside the same house! [98]

David knows that his own "live" ongoing bestseller - out of forty seven planned victims twenty three are already dead - is an outrageous media message worthy of his times, as well as a test of his own ability to deal with publicity: "it's all a question of keeping up with the times."[99] He assumes that his obsession is a valid reflection of contemporary civilization, in which the distinction between reality and imagination, between right and wrong, is blurred: "You take a thing which is real like this, and you know what? You say to yourself somebody is making it up!"[100]

Lish's novel suggests other moral and philosophical implications. Do the same impulses inspire both the writer and the criminal? Is killing in the pages of a book very different from killing in the streets of a city? Is being a killer a bit like being a novelist? "Both activities are forms of excommunication in which only one person lives to tell the tale," points out a critic.[101] David is convinced that clever phrasing or descriptions may serve as agents of depravity.

Vonnegut concurs. In *Breakfast of Champions*, the writer's persona, aware of being a transmitter of violence through fiction, comes to understand

how innocent and natural it was for them [Americans] to behave so abominably, and with such abominable results: They were doing their best to live like people invented in story books. This was the reason Americans shot each other so often: It was a convenient literary device for ending short stories and books.[102]

Alerting us to the various grim extensions of the power of writing and the accompanying mass-market sensationalism, Lish obliquely recognizes another possibility: authors themselves are uncannily inspired by their own, or other people's tormentors.* Many writer-characters and author-personae, including Garp, Zuckerman, Kosky, Barth, Roth, Exley, et al, concede, directly or indirectly, that they are as much fascinated as repelled by the perverts and maniacs around them. Even Bellow's Citrine is aware that there is a "natural connection" between him and the vicious gangster Cantabile. He muses: "How should I describe my feelings? Fear, thrill, appreciation, glee - yes I appreciated his ingenuity."[103]

Finally, an additional anxiety lurks in these themes of literature-related evil. Writer-heroes intimate that what they fear is that the psychopaths, the stalkers and assorted criminals that complicate their lives may be their only dedicated audience, that behind them lies a faceless, mindless public, a herd of increasingly illiterate consumers who may buy and read their books, but do not consider them relevant, or worthwhile. Moreover, they fear that publishers neglect sincere subjects and authors in favor of "soft," showbiz glitz; that the American public is becoming too busy, or too distracted, or too ignorant to read serious novels; that people are obsessed by the allure of the literary profession, or the charisma of writers, but remain indifferent to great themes, fascinating characters, innovative style.

Updike's Bech, in *Bech is Back*, realizes at one point he is a collector's item rather than a revered literary authority. When he visits Marvin Federbusch, the man who over many years conscientiously followed his career and systematically sent him copies of his publications for signing, Bech is dismayed to see a man who seems disturbed rather than pleased to meet the writer. Asked by Bech about the autographed books, Federbusch explains they are kept in a closet - "so the sun won't

---

*The theme is further explored by Lish in his collection of stories called *What I Know So Far* (1984).

fade the chackets" (sic) - and explains that they are an "inheritance" for his brother's children.

> The books were not erect in rows but stacked on their sides like lumber, like dubious ingots, in this lightless closet with - oh, treachery! - similarly exhaustive, tightly packed, and beautifully unread collections of Roth, Mailer, Barth, Capote....The closet door was shut before Bech could catalogue every one of the bedfellows the promiscuous Federbusch had captivated.[104]

Kosinski's Kosky deplores the fact that people know him not through his books but tv shows, which are spectacles of prime-time intellectual evasion. The celebrated "Controversy," a talk show on which Kosky's fiction is discussed, commands an audience of

> some sixteen million North American viewers aged anywhere between the ages of sixteen and ninety years, whose view of life, no longer dependent on reading books, has shifted to having them and their dead authors discussed live by two live'nd lively literati on the screen of their color TV, according to the *Literary TV Cable.*[105]

The novelist in John Williams' *!Click Song* deplores the fact that publishers want only fiction that follows the rationale of tv producers. His own publisher instructs him that "characters can't be subtle; they've gotta be up front and glamorous and tough and, yes, one-dimensional. That's just the way it's getting to be, Cate. No-*thinking.*"[106]

Beyond such complaints lurk fears that the print medium itself is doomed, outdated, consigned to dusty libraries. Writer-heroes suspect that writing as a profession is itself in jeopardy because people cease to read books, also because books are being replaced by technological innovation: electronic information systems, computer networks, data banks, texts as digits, disks, data transmissions. Reading fiction in its traditional form may soon expire along with the writer, Nadine Gordimer recently observed, because his "expectations of wider readership" diminish "in inverse proportion to the expansion of technological communications."[107] Kosky, in Kosinski's *The Hermit*, is told that "These days, all arts end up as video , not as *roman*," that soon "books will be written not in words but in predigested nonverbal images called up by a writer on a personal LIC - a literary image computer."[108] Prophetically, the early works of Burroughs (who has unexpectedly emerged as a pop-cultural icon of the 1990s) offer visions of life regulated by circuits, artificial intelligence, media bombardment, codes imposed on us by inhuman intelligence systems.

CONCLUSION

World War II brings abrupt discontinuity to writer-protagonists in American fiction. In the 1950s we deal with heroes whose lives are strangely shrunken, whose experiences are dulled, whose sense of history is painful and uneasy. In an unprecedented manner, they claim to be filled with anxiety and paralysis induced not by personal or artistic crises but by a profound sense of an ideological and moral vacuum, by existential anxiety, by alienation. Their ambitious literary projects are stillborn - or finally abandoned. Experiences remain undigested, unused as fictive material, elusive as art. The resolution of idea and form is not accomplished, nor are affinities between life and work established. Creative energies are thwarted, or misused.

In the early 1960s, however, protagonists find ways of balancing apathy and defeat with new forms of spiritual sustenance. They discover that falsehoods can be used as metaphors, confusion as source of unorthodox ideology or a new sense of personal awareness. They find strength in exploring extremism, irony, bitterness, in a "dialectic...between a despair which is intolerable and a set of mythologies, born of that despair, which are untenable, silly, even inhuman".[109] No longer burnt-out cases, they are now obsessional.

In the decades that follow, despite frustration and failure, American writer-heroes are increasingly attracted to new possibilities: verbal experimentation, parodic visions of history and society, the blurring of fact and fiction, breakthrough expressions of self-reflexivity and narcissism, surreal confession. Yet, in the attempt to juggle the illusions of truth, or the metaphors of disruption, they frequently experience artistic and ideological doubt, self-pity and dread, which lead to anxious, contradictory statements concerning human relations and the modern experience. The desire to perform as literary magicians (or tricksters) is haunted by the dark suspicion that imaginative possibilities are limited, finally arbitrary and invalid - even useless.

Suspended between urges and ambitions that are both private and public, counter-culture and socially approved, writer-heroes of the past three decades explore society's opposing possibilities, immerse themselves in bizarre confrontations and whimsical fantasies. They may act as both artistic/political rebels or as agents for fashionable, media-based demands and non-events. Their fascination with the excessive and the marginal, their search for the specters of modern history or their unveiling of contemporary sham and corruption are typically (if quixotically) offset by vigorous pronouncements of acceptance and idealistic affirmation. Their openness concerning "instant fame" and market success, no longer at odds with the writer's spiritual needs and prominence, is accompanied by a recognition of an ambiguous affiliation between art and violence, literary power and criminality.

Yet, these writer-heroes are neither defeated nor in retreat. They manage to balance their fears concerning the state of the society, or their art, with a hope that anomalies may enrich rather than destroy American culture, that strategies are more important than certainties, that mental/technological change may ultimately inspire writing rather than make it obsolete. Perennially interested in a miscellany of factors and causes of American experience, they refuse to engage any of them seriously, or for long. "There are not many American books or poems," Leon Wieseltier points out, "that read like they had to be written because otherwise the writer would, in one way or another, out of pleasure or pain, decay or die. By and large, American writers do not look or talk or write like pressured men and women."[110]

The loss or evasion of certainties has lead to unconventional creative strategies but also to a loss of urgency in interpretation. Writer-heroes are unwilling, or unable, to rationalize and explain what is happening around them, to formulate our lives, to comprehend the forces that entangle them, to hold comprehensive visions of society. Similarly, they are only casually and inconsequentially attached to the history of literary and intellectual undertakings - except, of course, their own. Having little concern for tradition, social or historical - though notable exceptions like the Holocaust or political repression obtain - scornful of foreign guidelines, or visions of the future, they turn inward. Here they often find themselves drifting and undefined. Though eager to be popular and necessary, they have little to explain, or explore, and they are reluctant to offer moral judgement.

These narcissistic writer-heroes of recent American fiction are clearly the children of their age. They are enthusiastic advertisers of skill, experts in immediacy, maestros of reduction specializing in the socially visible and the ostentatious, the voluptuous and the neurotic. The elements of irony and doubt in their thinking are nevertheless balanced with vitality and humor. The glamour and hazards of their search for success are explored along with their radical views of reality and their playful exploitation of language - with equal skill and vigor.

The world of the writer is revealed in contemporary American fiction with a sense of poise that is never far removed from incoherence, dislocation, artfulness. The story of how one writes in our time is typically a process rather than an inquiry, a celebration of personality, not an intellectual or artistic/aesthetic exploration. It has the qualities of a deft creation; it is slick, topical, entertaining, urgent and radical - an intense, self-mirroring and self-generating performance.

NOTES

1.Philip Roth, *The Facts*, p.194.

2.John Barth, *Lost in the Funhouse*, p.118.

3.John Updike, *Bech is Back*, pp.107-109.

4.John Updike, *Bech: A Book*, p.64.

5.John Updike, *Bech is Back*, p.15.

6.Ibid., p.3.

7.John Updike, *Bech: A Book*, p.140.

8.Ibid., p.64.

9.Bernard Malamud, *The Tenants*, p.13.

10.Ibid., p. 146.

11.Ibid., p.49.

12.Ibid., p.173.

13.Don DeLillo, *Mao II*, p.37.

14.Ibid., pp.36-37.

15.Ibid., p.200.

16.Gilbert Sorrentino, *Mulligan Stew*, pp.57-58.

17.Ibid., p.62.

18.Ibid., p.260-61.

19.Joseph Heller, *Good as Gold* (1979; New York: Pocket Books, 1980), p.3.

20.Ibid., p. 330.

21.Ibid., p.36.

22.Ibid., p.440.

23.Ibid., p.381.

24.Philip Roth, *The Anatomy Lesson*, p.85.

25.Truman Capote, *Music for Chameleons*, p.xii.

26.Truman Capote, *Answered Prayers* (1987, London: Abacus, 1988), pp.72, 64.

27.Ibid., p.73.

28.Blackmur, Richard, P., ed., *Henry James: the Art of the Novel* (New York: Scribner, Sons, 1937), p.54.

29.Zola, Emil, *The Experimental Novel and Other Essays*, translated by Belle M. Sherman (New York: The Cassell Publishing Company, 1893), p.127.

30.James Thomas Farrell, *Literature and Morality* (New York: Vanguard Press, 1945), p.73.

31.Sherwood Anderson in a letter to a reader who asked him to critique her stories. Quoted in Raymond Carver's "Fame Is No Good, Take It Away From Me," *The New York Times Book Review*, April 22, 1984.

32. Ernest Hemingway, *A Movable Feast* (New York: Scribner's, 1964), p.155.

33.Jack London, *Martin Eden* (New York: Amsco School Publ., 1971), p.150.

34.Ronald Sukenick, "Up From the Garret: Success Then and Now", *The New York Times*, January 27, 1985.

35.Elmer Rice, "The Industrialization of the Writer," *Saturday Review*, April 12, 1952.

36."How Writers Live," *Time*, January 10, 1955.

37.Ronald Sukenick, "Up From the Garret: Success Then and Now," *The New York Times*, January 27, 1985.

38. Norman Podhoretz, *Making It* (New York: Random House, 1967), pp.338, xi.

39.Ibid, pp.xv and xvii.

40.Ibid., p.XIII.

41.Ibid., p.352.

42.Norman Mailer, *Advertisements of Myself* (New York: Putnam, 1959), pp. 19, 241.

43.Norman Mailer, *The Armies of the Night*, pp.33, 24.

44."In America, fame is an open door," conversation with Leo Braudy, *U.S.News and World Report*, Oct. 6, 1986.

45.Jerzy Kosinski, *The Hermit of 69th Street*, pp.240-49.

46.Interview with Saul Bellow, *TriQuarterly*, Northwestern University, Spring/Summer 1985, p.634.

47. Susan Sontag in an interview by Charles Ruas, *Dialogue*, #71, 1, 1986, also in *Conversations with American Writers* by Charles Ruas.

48.W.H.Auden, "Henry James and the Artist in America," *Harper's*, July 1948.

49.Leon Wieseltier, "American letters: a rude vigour...," *The Times Literary Supplement*, September 15-21, 1989.

50.Leslie Fiedler, "Literature and Lucre," *The New York Times Book Review*, May 31, 1981.

51.Saul Bellow, *Humboldt's Gift*, p.3.

52.Ibid., pp.119, 12, 6, 159.

53.Ibid., pp.11, 161.

54.Ibid., p.477.

55.Ibid., p.163.

56.Ibid., p.107.

57.Ibid., p.118.

58.Ibid., p.107.

59.Frederick Exley, *A Fan's Notes* (New York: Harper and Row, 1968), p.35.

60.Ibid., p.45.

61.Ibid., pp.202, 224.

62.Frederick Exley, *Pages from a Cold Island* (New York: Random House, 1975), p.11.

63.Frederick Exley, *A Fan's Notes*, p.385.

64.Max Apple, *The Oranging of America* (1976, Harmondsworth: Penguin, 1981), pp.49-60.

180

65.Philip Roth, *The Ghost Writer*, p.94.

66.Philip Roth, *Zuckerman Unbound* (1981; Harmondsworth: Penguin, 1983), p.9.

67.Ibid., p.9.

68.James Joyce, *Finnegans Wake* (London: Faber and Faber, 1975), p.192.

69.Philip Roth, *Zuckerman Unbound*, pp.87-89.

70.Ibid., pp.89-90.

71.Ibid., untitled page following title page.

72.Ibid., p.118.

73.Philip Roth, *The Anatomy Lesson* (1983; New York: Fawcett Crest, 1984), p.25.

74.Ibid., p.114.

75.Ibid., pp.164-65.

76.Ibid., p.85.

77.Ibid., p.231.

78.Philip Roth, *Zuckerman Unbound*, p.11.

79.Philip Roth, *The Anatomy Lesson*, pp.54, 132.

80.John Updike, *Bech is Back*, pp.135, 148.

81.Ibid., pp.148-49.

82.Ibid., p.150.

83.Erica Jong, *How to Save Your Own Life* (1976; New York: Signet, New American Library, 1978), p.10.

84.Ibid., p.17.

85.Ibid., pp.243-44.

86.Vladimir Nabokov, *Look at the Harlequins!*, pp.23, 89.

87.Jong, Erica, *Fear of Flying*, p.153.

88.Don DeLillo, *Mao II*, p.196.

89.John Irving, *The World According to Garp*, p.169.

90.Philip Roth, *Zuckerman Unbound*, p.105.

91.Ibid., p.78.

92.Ibid., p.138.

93.Philip Roth, *The Counterlife*, p.169.

94.Gordon Lish, *Dear Mr. Capote* (New York: Scribner's Signature, 1986), p.4.

95.Ibid., pp.5-7.

96.Ibid., pp.4, 12.

97.Ibid., p.133.

98.Ibid., p.132.

99.Ibid., p.121.

100.Ibid., p.111.

101.David Seabrook, "What we write about when we write about Gordon Lish," in Graham Clarke, ed., *The New American Writing; Essays on American Literature Since 1970* (London: Vision Press, 1990), p.131.

102.Kurt Vonnegut, *Breakfast of Champions*, pp.209-10.

103.Saul Bellow, *Humboldt's Gift*, pp.91, 101.

104.John Updike, *Bech is Back*, p.9.

105.Jerzy Kosinski, *The Hermit of 69th Street*, pp.556-57.

106.John Williams, *!Click Song*, p.281.

107.Nadine Gordimer, "The Gap Between the Writer and the Reader," *The New York Review*, Sept.28, 1989.

108.Jerzy Kosinski, *The Hermit of 69th Street*, p.473.

109.Michael Wood in a review of Vonnegut's fiction, *New York Review of Books*, May 31, 1973.

110.Leon Wieseltier, "American Letters: a rude vigour," *The Times Literary Supplement*, Sept. 15-21, 1989.

WORKS CONSULTED

Adair, Gilbert. *The Death of the Author*. London: Heinemann, 1992.

Allen, Mary. *The Necessary Blankness: Women in Major American Fiction of the Sixties*. Urbana: University of Illinois Press, 1976.

Alter, Robert. *Partial Magic: The Novel as a Self-Conscious Genre*. Berkeley and Los Angeles: Unversity of California Press, 1975.

Baran, Bogdan. *Postmodernizm*. Krakow, inter esse, 1992.

Beebe, Maurice. *Ivory Towers and Sacred Founts: The Artist as Hero in Fiction from Goethe to Joyce*. New York: New York University Press, 1964.

Bienstock, Beverly Gray. "The Self-Conscious Artist in Contemporary American Fiction." Dissertation, University of California, 1973.

Blackmur, R.P. "The Artist as Hero: A Disconsolate Chimera." In *The Lion and the Honeycomb: Essays in Solicitude and Critique*. New York: Harcourt, Brace, 1955.

Bradbury, Malcolm. *The Modern American Novel*. New York: Oxford University Press, 1984.

Brooks, Van Wyck. "The Hero as Artist." In *Sketches in Criticism*. New York: E.P. Duton, 1932.

Brooks, Van Wyck. *The Writer in America*. New York: Dutto, 1953.

Cornillon, Susan K. *Images of Women in Fiction: Feminist Perspectives*. Bowling Green, Bowling Green Univ. Popular Press.

Edmondson, Elsie F. L. "The Writer as Hero in Important American Fiction Since Howells." Dissertation. The University of Michigan, 1954.

Federman, Raymond. *Surfiction, Fiction Now...and Tomorrow*. Chicago: The Swallow Press, 1975.

Federman, Raymond. "Self-Reflexive Fiction." In *Columbia Literary History of the United States*, ed. Emory Elliott. New York: Columbia Univ. Press, 1988.

Ford, Boris, ed. *American Literature*. London: Penguin, 1988.

Galloway, David G. *The Absurd Hero in American Fiction*. Austin: University of Texas Press, 1966.

Gingrich, Patricia, C. L. "The Writer as Hero; A Changing Ideal in the British Novel from 1832-1919." Dissertation, Wayne State Univ.: Detroit, Michigan, 1969.

Graff, Gerald. *Literature Against Itself: Literary Ideas in Modern Society*. Chicago and London: Chicago University Press, 1979.

Hassan, Ihab. *Selves at Risk: Patterns of Quest in Contemporary American Letters*. The University of Wisconsin Press, 1990.

Hendin, Josephine. *Vulnerable People: A View of American Fiction since 1945*. New York: Oxford University Press, 1978.

Huf, Linda. *A Portrait of the Artist as a Young Woman: The Writer as Heroine in American Literature*. New York: Ungar, 1983.

Janeway, Elizabeth. *The Writer's World*. New York: McGraw Hill, 1969.

Karl, Frederick R. *American Fictions 1940-1980: A Comprehensive History and Critical Evaluation*. New York: Harper and Row, 1983.

Kellman, Steven G. *The Self-Begetting Novel*. New York: Columbia University Press, 1980.

Klinkowitz, Jerome. *Literary Disruptions: The Making of a Post-Contemporary American Fiction*. Urbana: University of Illinois Press, 1975.

Klinkowitz, Jerome. *The Practice of Fiction in America: Writers from Hawthorne to the Present*. The Iowa State University Press, Ames, 1980.

Klinkowitz, Jerome. *Literary Subversions: New American Fiction and the Practice of Criticism*. Carbondale: Southern Illinois Univ. Press, 1985.

Kopcewicz, Andrzej and Sienicka, Marta. *Historia literatury Stanów Zjednoczonych w zarysie*. Warszawa: PIW, 1982.

Kutnik, Jerzy. *The Novel as Performance: The Fiction of Ronald Sukenick and Raymond Federman.*Carbondale:Southern Illinois University Press, 1986.

Lemon, Lee, T. *Portraits of Artists in Contemporary Fiction.* Lincoln: University of Nebraska Press, 1985.

Lodge, Davis. *The Novelist at the Crossroads.* Ithaca, N.Y.: Cornell University Press, 1971.

McHale, Brian. *Postmodernist Fiction.* New York and London: Methuen, 1987.

Miller, Norman. "The Self-Conscious Narrator-Protagonist in American Fiction since World War II." Dissertation, University of Wisconsin, 1972.

Podhoretz, Norman. *Making It.* New York: Random House, 1967.

Poirer, Richard. *The Performing Self.* New York: Oxford University Press, 1971.

Roth, Philip. *Reading Myself and Others.* New York: Farrar, Straus and Giroux, 1975.

Ruland, Richard and Bradbury, Malcolm. *From Puritanism to Postmodernism: A History of American Literature.* Harmondsworth: Penguin, 1992.

Semrau, Janusz. *American Self-Conscious Fiction of the 1960s and 1970s: Donald Barthelme, Robert Coover, Ronald Sukenick.* Poznan: Wydawnictwo Naukowe UAM, 1986.

Smith, Stan. *A Sadly Contracted Hero: The Comic Self in Post-war American Fiction.* London: British Association for American Studies, 1981.

Stewart, Grace. *A New Mythos: The Novels of the Artist as Heroine.* St. Albans: VT: Eden Press, 1978.

Sukenick, Ronald. *In Form: Digressions on the Act of Fiction.* Carbondale and Edwardsville: Southern Illinois University Press, 1985.

Tanner, Tony. *City of Words: American Fiction, 1950-1970.* New York: Harper and Row, Publishers, 1971.

Tanner, Tony. *Scenes of Nature, Signs of Men.* Cambridge: University Press, 1987.

Weinberg, Helen. *The New Novel in America: The Kafkan Mode in Contemporary Fiction.* Ithaca, N.Y.: Cornell University Press, 1970.

Winkelman, Aaron. "Authorial Presence in American Metafiction: the Novels of Coover, Federman, Sorrentino, and Sukenick." Dissertation, University of California, Los Angeles, 1986.

INDEX

192